SCIENCE AND THEOLOGY

Also by John Polkinghorne:

The Way the World Is (1983)
The Quantum World (1984)
One World (1986, reissued 1996)
Science and Creation (1988, reissued 1997)
Science and Providence (1989)
Reason and Reality (1991)
Science and Christian Belief/The Faith of a Physicist (1994)
Quarks, Chaos and Christianity (1994)
Beyond Science (1996)
Scientists as Theologians (1996)
Belief in God in an Age of Science (1998)

Science and Theology

An Introduction

John Polkinghorne

SPCK / FORTRESS PRESS

First published in Great Britain 1998
Society for Promoting Christian Knowledge
Holy Trinity Church
Marylebone Road
London NW1 4DU

First published in North America 1998
Fortress Press
Box 1209
Minneapolis
Minnesota 55440

British Library Cataloguing-in-Publication Data
A catalogue record for this book is available
from the British Library.

ISBN 0–281–05176–3

ISBN for Fortress Press edition

ISBN 0–8006–3153–6

Typeset by Wilmaset Ltd, Birkenhead, Wirral
Printed in Great Britain by
The Cromwell Press, Trowbridge, Wiltshire

Contents

To
the memory of my parents
and of
my brother Peter
and
my sister Ann

Introduction

In recent years, many courses on science and religion have been inaugurated in colleges and universities, often encouraged and supported by grants from the John Templeton Foundation. The last thirty years have seen a great deal of scholarly writing in this academic area, so there have been many texts to which such courses could make reference. However, in my view, there has not been a textbook available. By that I mean a single book that attempts the humble but useful task of surveying the whole intellectual scene in an even-handed manner, recording as clearly as possible the variety of issues under discussion, explaining the possible treatments they can receive, and surveying the opinions of those writers who have made significant contributions to the field.

The invitation to be a visiting professor and to give a course on science and theology at General Theological Seminary, New York, gave me the opportunity to attempt such an exercise in the classroom and that experience encouraged me to write the present volume. I offer it as a potential textbook in the rapidly growing area of science and religion studies.

The work is organized in a spiral fashion, starting with general considerations and then progressing inward to deal with more specific questions. The first chapter discusses the nature of science and the nature of theology, drawing certain methodological and epistemological comparisons between them and indicating possible modes of interaction between the two disciplines. It also considers two critical incidents (Galileo, Darwin) in the history of that interaction. The second chapter gives an account, in terms accessible to the non-specialist, of those aspects of the contemporary scientific understanding of the universe and its history that are of relevance to wider metaphysical discussion.

Chapter 3 is concerned with what may be said about one of the most important meeting points of scientific and theological insight: the nature of the human person. Issues of reductionism and holism, dualist or monist views of human nature, and the relationship between mind and brain, are all on the agenda. In our present stage of knowledge, no universally agreed

1

conclusions can be stated, but the varying approaches on offer are described and evaluated.

The fourth chapter is concerned with the nature of God as it is understood in the broad Western tradition. An issue of great importance is the assessment of a revived and revised natural theology that makes appeal to the given laws and circumstances of the cosmos, as discerned by science, and asks what metaquestions may arise, pointing beyond the narrowly scientific account alone. The result is a natural theology that aims to complement, rather then conflict with, scientific insight. The discussion then broadens to include consideration of a theology of nature, creation, and the implications of a world found to be the carrier of value. The arguments of this chapter are as consistent with deism as they are with theism, but Chapter 5 moves on in a specifically theistic direction by asking the question of how one could conceive of particular divine actions taking place in the orderly universe described by science. No topic has been of greater concern in the writings of the science and religion community in recent years than this one. The various approaches that have been made are described and the chapter includes a careful discussion of the possible relevance of quantum theory and chaos theory to an understanding of agency, both human and divine. Attention is also given to the difficult but essential topic of theodicy, facing the critical issues for religious belief that arise from the widespread prevalence of moral and physical evil in God's supposedly good creation.

The focus of the discourse narrows in Chapter 6 to a consideration of topics central to Christian belief. The approach of the chapter is by way of 'bottom-up thinking' (seeking to move from evidence to understanding in the quest for motivated belief), so that it constitutes a sketch of how someone with the habits of thought congenial to the scientific mind approaches Christian theological issues. These include belief in the resurrection of Christ, in the Trinity, and in a destiny beyond death.

The discussion opens out again in Chapter 7 to include a brief account of various ways in which the different world faith traditions might be understood to relate to each other, bearing in mind the perplexities that arise from their very different claims about the nature of the sacred. The suggestion is made that considering the traditions' relationships to scientific knowledge might provide a creative meeting point for mutual encounter.

In Chapter 8, some discussion is given of the ethical issues that arise from scientific discoveries. The brief treatment given aims at highlighting matters of principle rather than attempting detailed analyses and case studies, which would require another volume for their adequate discussion. The book concludes with a select but quite extensive and annotated

2

bibliography, laid out in such a way as to help students to pursue particular points through further reading.

I have sought to give a balanced account of the many issues currently under discussion in the lively exchange across the intellectual frontier between science and theology. In fact, in the attempt to maintain a certain degree of impartiality, I have adopted the somewhat eerie practice of referring to myself in the third person on those occasions when I make specific references to my own ideas. Each chapter is written in a self-contained fashion, so that it should easily be possible to use the book for a course that did not aim to cover all the material here presented. For example, if it was not intended to give attention to specifically Christian issues, Chapter 6 could be omitted without doing violence to the rest of the text.

I regard the question of how the insights of science and the insights of religion can both be taken seriously, with intellectual integrity and openness, as being among the most important issues on the contemporary agenda. I offer this book as a contribution to the discussion of that great question.

I wish to thank my wife Ruth for her help in correcting the proofs.

1

The Area of Interaction

Every time we switch on the television, or use our PCs for work or pleasure, we are making use of facilities afforded us by the advance of science. Many of us are only alive today because medical discoveries enabled us to recover from illness which in past times would have proved fatal. The colossal sales of a book like Stephen Hawking's *Brief History of Time* show that there is a widespread yearning to understand what science can tell us of the history and structure of our universe. Yet there are other questions which nag at us, and which seem meaningful and necessary to ask, but in reply to which an honest science has to be silent. Is there a purpose behind the fifteen-billion-year sweep of cosmic history or do things just happen in a world devoid of ultimate meaning? Is reality in some sense 'on our side', or do we live in a cold and hostile universe? Is death the end or can we hope for a destiny beyond it? These are questions to which religion has traditionally given answers. We have to ask whether these answers, or something like them, are still available to us today. In an age of science, can we with integrity also take religion with the utmost seriousness? Are science and religion conflicting or complementary? That is the broad issue for our investigation.

Some Historical Incidents

We form in a variety of ways the concepts which are the tools of our thought. Logical analysis is only a part of the process, for we also make use of the imaginative resource of story. Many people's attitude to science and religion is powerfully affected by two narratives, both of which appear to carry the message of a truth-seeking science confronting an obscurantist and conservative religion. These are the modern myths of Galileo and Charles Darwin, both seen as being in conflict with the Church. In the form in which these stories are deposited in contemporary minds they are presented as simple accounts of the battle of light with darkness, an impression sedulously fostered by their re-presentation in the

4

media from time to time. In actual fact, the truth is altogether more complex and correspondingly more interesting.

Galileo

Born in 1564, Galileo Galilei is unquestionably one of the great figures in the history of science. He repudiated mere appeal to the authority of Aristotle and in its place pioneered the investigative technique of combining mathematical argument with an appeal to observation and experiment. His brilliant use of the newly discovered telescope as a means for searching the heavens (resulting in the discovery of mountains on the Moon, spots on the Sun, satellites encircling Jupiter, and the phases of Venus) reinforced his belief in the Copernican system. By 1616 this had got him into trouble with the Vatican authorities, who believed that the Ptolemaic system, with its fixed Earth, was endorsed by the Bible. Some kind of accommodation was worked out between Galileo and his chief critic, Cardinal Bellarmine. The exact terms of this agreement later became a matter of dispute and there is a continuing scholarly debate on the question. The point at issue is whether Galileo was simply told not to espouse or defend the Copernican principle or whether he was also forbidden to teach it in any way whatsoever. Whatever the rights of the matter, intellectual freedom was clearly curtailed by the exercise of ecclesiastical authority.

In 1632, Galileo published his *Dialogue Concerning the Two Chief World Systems*. Cast in the apparent form of an even-handed discussion of the pros and cons of the ideas of Ptolemy and Copernicus, its actual presentation of the case for Copernicanism was so overwhelming that it was clearly a tract in that system's defence. Moreover, Simplicio, the defender of Ptolemy, was not only weak in argument and something of a buffoon, but he also stated, almost word for word, points of view which had been propounded by the current pope, Urban VIII. It is scarcely surprising that the authorities were upset and they responded by summoning Galileo to appear before them. He was sentenced by the Inquisition to life imprisonment, immediately commuted by the Pope to continuing house arrest. At no stage was Galileo subjected to torture.

No one can claim that this is an edifying story or that the church authorities displayed wisdom or intellectual integrity in their implacable opposition to Galileo's Copernican ideas. (The Roman Catholic ban on Copernicanism was rescinded in 1820 but Galileo's condemnation was only recently abrogated formally.) Yet the issues were complex and the illumination afforded by hindsight should not result in our painting the scene in stark black and white. There were scientific difficulties in the case presented by Galileo. One was the absence of stellar parallax – the shift in the apparent position of the stars expected to result from their being viewed from different perspectives if the Earth were moving round an orbit in the course of the year. (We now know that this was not observable with seventeenth-century resources because the stars are so very distant from us.) Galileo placed great emphasis on the claimed confirmatory value of his explanation of the tides. We now know that he was completely in error about this matter. He even ridiculed Kepler when the latter suggested that the Moon might have some relevance for tidal phenomena!

Throughout the controversy, and until his death, Galileo remained a religious man. Many of his discussions with his opponents had focused on the right way in which to read the Bible. Galileo genuinely valued its spiritual authority, but the fact that it was written in language intended to be understood by common people meant, in his opinion, that it was illegitimate to try to read advanced physical theory out of its pages. If there was an apparent conflict between the surface meaning of words of Scripture and the results of science, Galileo believed that this should encourage us to seek a deeper understanding of the relevant biblical passage – a view for which he could appeal to the support of St Augustine, no less.

Cardinal Bellarmine had urged upon Galileo the view that mathematical theories, like that of Copernicus, were just means of 'saving the appearances', that is to say that they were calculational devices and not necessarily to be taken seriously as literal descriptions. Here we have an engagement with one of the fundamental questions in the philosophy of science, to which we shall subsequently return. Are scientific theories just convenient 'manners of speaking', or do they describe the physical world as it actually is?

Finally, there were the personal aspects of the controversy: Urban VIII's wounded pride, Galileo's brilliant but polemically sharp use of the Italian language, the ambitions of Galileo's opponents among the Jesuit astonomers (to this day effective participants in the scientific community). These varied considerations do not mean that the Roman Catholic authorities did not make a bad mistake. Of course they did, but in complex and cloudy circumstances. The Galileo affair by no means indicates that there is an inevitable incompatibility between science and religion. One unwise incident does not imply a continuing conflict.

Darwin

But do we not see the same thing happening all over again following the publication in 1859 of Charles Darwin's *Origin of Species*? Once more popular myth presents a picture of light confronting darkness. The image of Galileo before the Inquisition is succeeded by the image of Thomas Huxley vanquishing Bishop Samuel Wilberforce in their debate at the Oxford meeting of the British Association for the Advancement of Science in 1860. The story goes that the bishop was unwise enough to enquire of Huxley whether he was descended from an ape via his grandfather or his grandmother. Such a tasteless tactic brought the stern rebuke that Huxley would rather have an ape for an ancestor than a bishop who was unwilling to face the truth.

There is, in fact, some doubt about what actually happened on this occasion. Huxley's own version was put on paper thirty years after the event and the contemporary accounts are by no means unanimous in recounting a famous victory by the scientist. Be that as it may, once again the full story is more complex and confused than myth allows.

At the scientific level, there were contemporary biological critics of the idea of evolution by natural selection, like Sir Richard Owen, the greatest anatomist of the day, who pointed to difficulties in Darwin's thesis. Indeed Wilberforce himself, who was genuinely interested in scientific matters, wrote a review of the *Origin* which Darwin acknowledged as making some telling points in relation to the problems faced by the theory. The great British physicists of the nineteenth century, such as Faraday, Maxwell and Stokes, were silent in public but privately had doubts about the unaided adequacy of natural selection to explain the development of life in the timescale available. Lord Kelvin broke that silence when he claimed that the rate of the Earth's cooling and the length of the era during which the Sun could have been shining restricted the time available to a period much shorter than that required by Darwin's theory. While Kelvin's calculations were correct in terms of the known physics of his day, he was unaware of the processes of radioactivity (which has had a significant warming effect upon the Earth) and nuclear fusion (which has powered the Sun for the five billion years of its shining).

If the scientific scene was confused, so was the religious. At the very same meeting of the British Association which had seen the debate between Wilberforce and Huxley, Frederick Temple (later to be Archbishop of Canterbury) preached a sermon welcoming the insights of evolution. There was by no means uniform opposition to Darwin's ideas from within the Church. Charles Kingsley took a robust view of accepting scientific truth and insight, seeing natural selection as relating to the 'how' of God's creative action and interpreting evolution as replacing the notion of the Creator's instant act by the subtler and more satisfying idea of a creation brought into being and able then to 'make itself'. One of Darwin's friends and regular correspondents, Asa Gray the Harvard

7

botanist, did much to make evolution a respectable idea among thinking people in North America, while remaining a deeply religious man.

Once again, there were personal factors at work, influencing the behaviour of the participants. Wilberforce may have wanted to stand on episcopal dignity, but Thomas Huxley was also strongly motivated by non-intellectual considerations, such as the desire to reduce the traditional influence of the clergy and to establish the authority of the newly emerging class of professional scientists. Charles Darwin's own loss of the Christian belief he had held as a young man is thought to have been at least as much influenced by sadness at the harrowing death of his daughter Annie at the age of ten, as by his scientific discoveries. In assessing Darwin's later cautious utterances on religion one must remember his sensitive wish not to offend his wife Emma, who was a person of religious faith, but he never became an out-and-out atheist. Even Huxley did not go as far as explicit atheism, coining the word 'agnostic' to describe those who, like himself, felt the question of God's existence to be beyond settlement.

Conclusion

Rightly read, the Galileo and Darwin incidents are instructive and focused examples of how religion and science can interact. In each case, certain beliefs previously held by all people (the centrality of the Earth, the immutability of species) proved to be in need of radical revision. Because theological thinking had incorporated these common notions into its background assumptions, it too had to make changes in how it understood its insights to relate to other forms of knowledge. This was not a comfortable process for theology. In each case there was initial resistance, but this was by no means total. At the same time, the scientific case was not itself immediately crystal clear and arguments persisted for a while, since radical revision is no more easy for scientists than it is for theologians. Yet in the end the dust settled for both subjects. Theology discovered that the dignity of humankind depended neither upon its inhabiting the centre of the universe nor upon *Homo sapiens* being a separately and instantaneously created species.

Some scholars have even suggested that, far from science and religion being at enmity with each other, it was the Judaeo-Christian-Islamic concept of the world as creation that enabled science to flower in seventeenth-century Europe, rather than in ancient Greece or medieval China, despite the great intellectual achievements of these latter two civilizations. The doctrine of creation implies that:

- the world is orderly, since God is rational;
- no prior constraints are imposed on the Creator's choice of creation's pattern, so that one has to look (observe and experiment) to see what the divine will has selected;
- because creation is not itself sacred, it can be investigated without impiety;
- because the world is God's creation, it is a worthy object of study.

Certainly the search for order through experimental investigation is fundamental to the practice of science and not all religious cultures would provide encouragement to this task.

We shall return to some of these themes in what follows, but first we must set the scene for a more systematic discussion of the interaction between science and theology by giving careful consideration to what is the actual nature of these two forms of intellectual enquiry.

The Nature of Science

Many people have in their minds a picture of how science proceeds which is altogether too simple. This misleading caricature portrays scientific discovery as resulting from the confrontation of clear and inescapable theoretical predictions by the results of unambiguous and decisive experiments. The perfect matching of the two is then held to establish unassailable scientific truth. In actual fact, once again, the reality is more complex and more interesting than that.

Complications

The following considerations need to be taken into account.

No clear separation can be made between theory and experiment. This is because all scientifically interesting facts are already interpreted facts. Understanding the way measuring instruments work depends upon theories of how they function. In a modern experiment investigating the behaviour of subatomic particles, the raw data correspond to flashes of light or discharged sparks in the interiors of sophisticated pieces of detecting apparatus. The translation of these macroscopic events into a story of the interactions of microscopic entities requires reliance upon a detailed understanding of the properties and electromagnetic interactions of the particles believed to be present.

Scientists do not look at the world with a blank gaze; they view it from a chosen perspective and bring principles of interpretation and prior expectations of meaning to bear upon what they observe. Scientists wear (theoretical) 'spectacles behind the eyes' (Russell Hanson). They may decide that the prescription for those spectacles needs changing from time to time – science is corrigible – but without some such interpretative aid the practice of science would be impossible. The problems that this poses are at least as old as Galileo. His opponents suggested that the mountains he claimed to see on the Moon were distortions induced by his newfangled telescope.

Experimental vision is clouded by the complexity of what is going on, with the consequent difficulty of being sure that one is actually focusing on the phenomena one wishes to observe. Among scientists, this is called the problem of 'background'. Many effects (friction, purity of the sample, temperature fluctuations, competing processes, etc.) can contaminate the interaction being studied and so distort the character of the results observed. These unwanted effects must be eliminated or allowed for. Their identification depends upon the scientist's accumulated experience of what might go wrong. Their estimation depends upon theoretical insight. There is no infallible guide to what might happen. Allowance for background effects requires the exercise of skilled personal judgement by the experimenter.

Scientific theories purport to make assertions about what happens everywhere and at all times. They have universal intent, but they can be based only on finite experience. However extensive that experience might be, it cannot cover

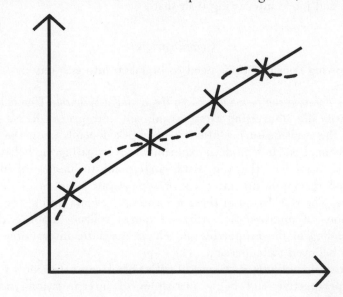

all possibilities. In a blunt word, theories are underdetermined by experiment. This underdetermination might lead to two errors: incorrect interpolation or incorrect extrapolation. The former is concerned with filling in a realm of experience already crudely surveyed. The points in the figure (opposite page) seem to fall on a straight line but closer investigation might reveal that actually they are connected by a wavy curve. This can be tested by more detailed investigation, but there will always be some gaps left unfilled. The second error results when changing the scale to something much larger proves to reveal an unexpected change in behaviour. The 'straight line' in the figure might be a very shallow curve whose shape would only become apparent when points are measured far outside the range shown.

Radical revisions do in fact occur in science from time to time when a new regime is opened up to investigation by proceeding, say, to higher energy or lower temperature than ever before. The two great discoveries of twentieth-century physics – quantum theory and relativity theory – were brought to light in just this way. It was found that when one moved from the world of everyday events to phenomena occurring on the scale of atoms or less (10^{-8} cm or smaller) the clear and determinate world described by Newtonian theory dissolved into the cloudy and fitful behaviour characteristic of quantum theory. Similarly, when particles move with velocities comparable to the velocity of light (3.10^{10} cm/sec), their mass is no longer found to be constant but it increases with increasing velocity.

Thomas Kuhn built a whole philosophy of science around this kind of radical change, which he referred to as a 'paradigm shift'. The word 'paradigm' is meant to represent a comprehensive point of view from which one surveys the nature of reality. There is the Newtonian paradigm in which, for instance, mass is an unvarying measure of the amount of matter, and there is the Einsteinian paradigm in which mass is a quantity that depends upon matter's particular state of motion. At his most extreme, Kuhn claimed that these two views were incommensurable; that they were so different that in a conversation between Isaac (Newton) and Albert (Einstein) each would not be able to understand what the other was talking about. Later, calmer thoughts modified this assertion.

Certainly, such revolutionary changes imply that science cannot claim the achievement of final truth. It must always remain open to the possibility of a radical revision of parts of its story. Yet Einstein modified Newton rather than abolishing him. We can readily understand Newton's classical mechanics as being a limiting case of relativistic mechanics, apt enough for the case where velocities are all small compared to that of light. Scientific theories can be thought of as constituting maps of the

11

physical world. No map ever represents everything that might be said about the terrain. Changing the scale may well reveal new and unexpected features. Yet maps are superposable; we can understand how they relate to each other.

An important concept is that of 'charitable reference'. Two people can be recognized as talking about the same thing without demanding that they understand precisely the same things about it. When Newton and Einstein refer to mass they both are concerned with inertia, a body's resistance to having its state of motion changed. I think that Isaac would be very interested to learn how Albert discovered that this quantity actually varies with speed.

Science is practised within the community of scientists. As with every society, this implies that there are communal expectations and ways of thinking which are all the more influential for being tacit rather than explicit. These social effects certainly affect scientific discovery.

Let me give an example. Until the 1950s it was thought obvious that nature would be even-handed, that is to say, that there would be no fundamental processes that were intrinsically right-handed or intrinsically left-handed. Of course, there could be 'handed' entities, such as cork-screws, but that is because of the way in which they have been put together and not as a result of the nature of their basic constituents. It is as easy to make a left-handed corkscrew as a right-handed one. There were certain reasonably straightforward experiments that could have been done to check whether this supposed fundamental even-handedness held in a subatomic domain. No one bothered to do them because it was thought that the answer would be boringly obvious. In 1956, two physicists, C. N. Yang and T. D. Lee, gave excellent theoretical reasons for questioning this belief. The socially induced experimental stupor was broken and it was soon discovered that there was an intrinsic handedness in certain subatomic events.

This story illustrates how social factors can affect the rate of scientific discovery, but it does not show that the form of that discovery, when it comes, is socially moulded. Once people got round to doing the experiments, the answer was unambiguous. There are, however, sociologists of knowledge who have seemed to claim the contrary. It is suggested that the invisible college of scientists reaches certain conclusions, less because nature actually takes this particular form, but because the college has unconsciously decided to describe nature in this way. Most scientists reject such a strong role for social forces in their discipline. The physical world does not seem to them to be so plastic in their encounter with it that they can twist its patterns into shapes that please their intellectual fancy. On the contrary, nature often resists our prior expectations and the eventual discovery, when it comes, is frequently very surprising, beyond our powers to have anticipated beforehand. (The discovery of quantum theory was an extreme example of this kind.)

Some Responses

The considerations just described mean that some subtlety is necessary in describing what science is about and how it discharges its task. In contemporary philosophy of science a number of responses have been made.

The minimal view of science is that it is simply *a means of 'saving the appearances'*, of giving an account whose principal object is to produce results in agreement with experiment without being concerned whether it is describing the physical world 'as it really is'. This was the view urged upon Galileo by Cardinal Bellarmine, and it is the view of a contemporary empiricist like Bas van Fraassen who thinks that we should accept science but not believe it. The most extreme examples of this approach were the positivists of the Vienna school, who thought that science was simply concerned with the correlation of basic sense perceptions. A big difficulty for this minimalist approach is that it seems quite inadequate to motivate scientific endeavour or give an adequate account of scientific experience. Much empirical evidence in physics is obtained from highly contrived and special circumstances which scientists have set up artificially. This labour, so expensive of time, talents and money, seems quite pointless if it is not a vehicle for the investigation of what the physical world is actually like. We have already noted that the pursuit of science is full of surprises as physical reality resists our prior expectations. The feel of this activity is the feel of discovery. Scientists are driven by the desire to understand and not simply by the ability to correlate or predict accurately. The philosophical description of science must be congruent with the experience of its practitioners.

Many contemporary philosophers would respond by saying that science has sufficient point if it enables us (as it undoubtedly does) to get things done. For them, *pragmatism* is the name of the game. Technology is not just a useful spin-off from science but it is, in their view, science's defining achievement. This flies in the face of the desire for understanding, not practical success, that motivates almost all pure scientists.

The inadequacy of pragmatism can be illustrated by a parable. A black box is delivered at the Meteorological Office with the instructions, 'Feed in details of today's weather through slot A, turn the handle, and out of slot B will come the correct prediction of the weather in a week's time.' It seems unlikely, but the meteorologists give it a go. Behold, it always works! The pragmatic task of the Met. Office is now perfectly fulfilled, but we may be sure that the scientists there would not all pack up and go home. Soon they would be taking that black box to pieces to see how it worked. Their desire is not simply to predict the weather but to understand it.

Finally, pragmatism also leaves unexplained whence science derives its marvellous power to manipulate the world so successfully. Far and away the most natural explanation is that it derives from science's knowledge of what the world is actually like.

Karl Popper was primarily a logician. He despaired of solving the problem of induction, of justifying how a completely general theory could be based on a limited number of specific tests. Ultimate verification seemed beyond the reach of finite experience. Instead, Popper saw that falsification required only one counterexample: 'All swans are white' – until the first sighting of a black swan in Australia. So, for Popper, the characteristic feature of science is its *falsifiability*. He believed its method to be the making of bold conjectures which are then open to empirical refutation. At first sight, this proposal seems attractive. One experiment was enough to dispose of the theory of the even-handedness of subatomic processes. Popper undoubtedly put his finger on an important aspect of scientific practice, but further reflection shows that he succeeded in telling only a part of the story.

There are two big problems with the Popperian view, both arising from reflection on the actual history of science. The first is that, according to Popper, the only real knowledge that the scientist ever acquires is knowledge of error rather than knowledge of truth. We know that 'All swans are white' is false but we do not know what true statement to make about the colour of swans. (We cannot logically dispose of the possibility of a turquoise one turning up.) Yet surely, in actual fact, we have learned some things scientifically that we are never going to have to revise. Atoms have come to stay, and so has the helical structure of DNA. Popper cannot account for this gain in knowledge. The second difficulty is that falsification is not as straightforward a concept as one might suppose. This is the case even for a low-level theory such as the whiteness of swans. (That Western Australian bird might be a long-necked duck.) When it comes to high-level theories, like Newton's theory of gravity, the problem of refutation is much more complex. When the planet Uranus did not appear to be behaving as the theory predicted, astronomers did not abandon inverse square law gravity as a discredited theory. Instead,

14

they supposed that there must be a further planet, not yet discovered, which was perturbing the Uranian orbit. The eventual discovery of Neptune was a triumphant vindication of this point of view.

Imre Lakatos sought to modify Popper's ideas in order to take these historical considerations into account. He conceived the notion of a *research programme*. This scientific endeavour is characterized by its hard core, the non-negotiable basic assumptions that specify its definition. For the Newtonian programme, the hard core would be universal inverse square law gravity. This is buffered from direct contact with experimental results by a protective belt of auxiliary hypotheses that are capable of alteration in order to preserve the core inviolate. For the Newtonian programme, one auxiliary hypothesis would be the number and nature of the planets composing the solar system. It is permissible to adjust this hypothesis by assuming the existence of an extra planet. The discovery of Neptune then represents a stunning and dramatic success for the programme that earns for it the epithet 'progressive'. However, there may come a time when the cost of the auxiliary hypotheses necessary to save the core becomes excessive. The programme has then become 'degenerative' and a new programme must be sought. This happened eventually to the Newtonian programme when it was replaced by Einstein's programme because the latter had a superior ability to afford an economical explanation of the detailed behaviour of the planet Mercury. Lakatos has clearly succeeded in giving a more persuasive account than that provided by Popper, but there remains the question of how one hits upon the research programme that will represent the next progressive step.

This was precisely the sort of problem discussed by *Michael Polanyi*, who was a distinguished physical chemist before he turned to philosophical pursuits. His ideas have largely been neglected by professional philosophers but they resonate with scientists, who recognize in Polanyi someone who knew their discipline from within. His central thesis is that, though science is concerned with the impersonal physical world, its pursuit is an *activity of persons*. The scientific method cannot be reduced to a well-formulated protocol whose execution could be delegated to a computer. Instead, it involves tacit skills of judgement (in relation to such issues as the elimination of background effects, sufficiency of confirming evidence, naturalness of theory choice, etc.) which are not capable of exhaustive codification and which represent skills learned through example by serving an apprenticeship in the 'convivial' community of scientists.

In a phrase that he often repeated, Polanyi believed that 'We know more than we can tell'. Discoveries involve creative acts of the human

15

imagination. Scientists do not just draw a bow at a refutable venture but there is a skilful selection of lines to pursue, based both on intuition and on experience. There is an indispensable role in science for the creative person, whose individual proposals are, nevertheless, offered with universal intent to be judged and sifted within the competent community of scientific peers. Polanyi called his understanding of science 'personal knowledge'. He sought to do justice both to the precarious boldness of scientific thought, and also to the experienced success with which the venture is conducted.

Critical Realism

The occasional occurrence of radical revision in scientific theory-making means that one cannot claim the achievement of science to be that of the attainment of absolute truth. However, we have seen that there is sufficient continuity of understanding across the boundaries of paradigm shifts to be able to interpret science's development as resulting in a tightening grasp of physical reality, the making of better and better maps of the physical world. In a word, science can claim verisimilitude, the attainment of increasingly closer approximations to the truth about physical process. A measure of that closeness is afforded by the range and character of phenomena brought within the scope of understanding. Quantum theory explains all that Newtonian mechanics could explain and much more besides.

The underdetermination of theory by experiment means that science is not just read out directly from nature but its progress involves creative acts by thinking minds. Non-empirical criteria, such as economy and naturalness, are important discriminators between competing suggestions and in practice they ae found to lead to unique proposals. The satisfaction of these criteria involves personal judgement but the choice is not a mere matter of whimsical taste, for the experience of scientists is that the theories selected in this way prove themselves by their long-term fertility, their power to explain phenomena going way beyond the scope of those whose consideration gave rise to the idea in the first place.

For example, the physicist Paul Dirac formulated an equation which succeeded in combining quantum theory with special relativity in a consistent fashion. An immediate, but unanticipated, bonus from the discovery of this equation was that it was found to imply that the magnetic interactions of electrons were twice what one would naively have expected them to be. This was already known to be the case but no one previously had been able to understand why it was so. A few years later, more thinking about the same equation led Dirac to the fundamental discovery of the existence of antimatter. Such continuing and uncovenanted fruitfulness is very persuasive that one is on to something of real significance.

Acts of personal judgement, of the kind discussed by Polanyi, are also involved in experimental assessment, as well as in theory choice. They are necessary, for example, in the identification and assessment of competing background effects.

Finally, the intertwining of theory and experiment gives a certain degree of circularity to scientific argument. If entities behave in the way that theory supposes, then this is what is happening in this experiment; if this is what is happening, then this is the appropriate theory to describe what is going on. The increase in understanding of physical process afforded by cumulative scientific advance can be appealed to as a sign that this circularity is benign and not vicious.

The account of science and its achievements which this subsection has sketched is called 'critical realism'. It is a realist position because it claims the attainment of increasingly verisimilitudinous knowledge of the nature of the physical world. It is a critical realist position because that knowledge is not directly obtained by looking at what is going on, but it requires a subtle and creative interaction between interpretation and experiment. This acknowledgement of somewhat oblique discernment gives science a degree of kinship with other forms of human enquiry. Science is not perceived as dealing with clear and indubitable facts, while other disciplines have to be content with cloudy opinions. On the contrary, all human knowledge is personal knowledge, though science's power to manipulate the object of its investigation and to put it to the experimental test gives it a technique of confirmation not available in other realms of experience, such as personal encounter, where the integrity of the other demands a greater degree of restrained respect.

One could not predict beforehand that science would be possible, that its logically precarious circularity would lead to unique and intellectually satisfying understandings of the physical world of such a kind as to be persuasive that one is actually learning about the nature of things. Yet that is what the history of modern science exemplifies. Critical realism is a philosophical position based on the actual experience of the scientific community, rather than on a claimed abstract necessity that things had to be this way. This basis in experience is why it is the position adopted, consciously or unconsciously, by the overwhelming majority of working scientists, despite the criticisms levelled at it by some of their philosophical colleagues.

The Nature of Theology

Just as the object of scientific enquiry is the physical world, so the object of theological enquiry is God. However, such a statement only carries one a little way into an understanding of the nature of theology. The difficulty is that most of us in Europe and North America can more or less agree what we are talking about when we refer to the physical world, but God is a different kind of being altogether, concerning whose character and credibility there is a great deal of disagreement. Some discussion of the nature of God as understood in the Judaeo-Christian-Islamic tradition will be attempted in a later chapter. For the present, it will be sufficient to emphasize that mainstream theology has never thought of God in terms of an important but invisible actor on the stage of the world but rather as the Author and Producer of the cosmic play. God is party to all that happens but not necessarily the immediate cause of all that happens. Part of the difficulty in discerning the divine presence is that no creature has ever experienced divine absence. This does not mean, however, that God is equally readily discernible in every event, for there may be particular happenings or particular people who are especially transparent to the divine presence. Gravity is always at work, but when Isaac Newton reflected on the fall of an apple he became aware of it in a special way. So it may be with the encounter with God, that there are revelatory events of prime significance which provide theology with the basic phenomena it seeks to understand.

Theological Discourse

George Lindbeck has suggested that there are three distinct approaches to the practice of theology.

The first is labelled 'cognitive'. Lindbeck regards its characteristic style as being the statement of propositions about God. Because of the feebleness of finite human minds in confronting the infinite mystery of the divine, the principal source of this carefully stated knowledge must be expected to be God's gracious acts of self-disclosure. Revelation is the record of such moments of divine unveiling, and Scripture and tradition preserve the experience that is accumulated in this way. There is some kinship between this understanding of theology and the unproblematic accounts of science's encounter with the physical world that were current before there had been a due appreciation of the subtle interweaving of theory and experiment actually involved in the practice of science. Some Christian theologians of the past sought a correspondingly unproblematic biblical basis for their thinking. Today it seems necessary to attempt a more nuanced approach to the use of Scripture, recognizing that it contains material anchored in the thought of the age in which it was written as well as material that transcends those cultural limitations.

The second approach is labelled 'experiential-expressive'. Science involves an impersonal encounter with the world, treating reality as an object (an 'it'), but religion has an indispensable personal and value-laden dimension to it (a meeting with a 'thou'). In this second approach, theological discourse is regarded as centring on the expression of those inner attitudes that serve as the basis for the way we live our lives. The statement 'God is love' is interpreted as the assertion of the primacy of loving relationships. When people treat the adjective 'Christian' as being equivalent to the adjective 'kind', they are adopting this way of theological thinking. The approach has a considerable degree of kinship with the pragmatic understanding of science, treated as a means to a desirable end. Thus the idea of God is held to symbolize in a useful way for us what is involved in our highest individual ideals.

The third approach is labelled 'cultural-linguistic'. Theology is held to be about the specification of an authoritative guide to communal action and discourse. It provides the framework within which we should live our lives and the perspective from which we should evaluate our experience. There is kinship here with the Kuhnian notion of a scientific paradigm, the viewpoint from which we survey the physical world. Religion provides the community with a shared pattern for living.

Like the accounts of science with which they have been compared, these characteristics of the nature of theological discourse each contain an element of truth, but one which becomes dangerously distorting if it is mistaken for a totally adequate description. Theological understanding certainly ought to be concerned with discerning what is the case and with the quest for truth about divine reality, but the cognitive approach, with its propositional style, is in danger of being altogether too cut and dried in the rationally self-confident way in which it presumes to talk about God's veiled presence. Theological understanding certainly ought to lead to the pursuit of a way of life based on love, but it can only urge that with integrity if it is truly the case that at the heart of reality is One who loves. The experiential-expressive approach is in danger of becoming a sentimental moralism. Theological understanding certainly has to be pursued within the tradition of a community, yet that tradition is not self-authenticating but it derives its authority from the belief that it is the fitting response to the One who stands over that community in mercy and judgement. The cultural-linguistic approach is in danger of degenerating into a mere endorsement of 'the way we do things'.

As with science, so even more with theology, the search for verisimilitudinous knowledge is subtle and manifold. Its character cannot be reduced to a simple, flat description. For both disciplines, critical realism provides a concept that both acknowledges that there is a truth to be found and also recognizes that the finding of that truth is not achievable through the application of some straightforward and specifiable technique. Both disciplines are concerned with the search for motivated belief and their understandings originate in interpreted experience. The necessary circularity involved in this process is no surprise or embarrassment to theology. Since Augustine, it has known that one must believe in order to understand and understand in order to believe.

Science does not have a privileged route of access to knowledge through some superior 'scientific method', uniquely its own possession; theology does not have a privileged route of access to knowledge through some ineffable source of unquestionable 'revelation', uniquely its own possession. Both are trying to grasp the significance of their encounters with manifold reality. In the case of science, the dimension of reality concerned is that of a physical world that we transcend and that can be put to the experimental test. In the case of theology, it is the reality of God who transcends us and who can be met with only in awe and obedience. Once that distinction is understood, we can perceive the two disciplines to be intellectual cousins under the skin, despite the differences arising from their contrasting subject material.

Varieties of Interaction

If science and theology really are, as has been claimed, partners in the great human quest to understand reality, then they are capable of interacting with each other. Ian Barbour has offered a useful classification of the various kinds of interactions that might arise.

Conflict

This occurs when either discipline threatens to take over the legitimate concerns of the other. Examples would be scientism (the assertion that the only meaningful questions to ask or possible to answer are scientific questions, thus claiming to abolish theological discourse altogether) or biblical literalism (the assertion that Genesis 1 and 2 provide an account of the origin of the universe and of life to which the scientific story must be made to conform in detail). Such totalitarian views of the scope of either science or theology have scant plausibility, being based on gross oversimplifications of the complexity and range of actual human knowledge and experience.

Independence

This stance treats science and theology as being quite separate realms of enquiry in which each discipline is free to pursue its own way without reference to, or hindrance by, the other. A frequent expression of this point of view is in terms of a series of dichotomies: science asks 'How?', religion asks 'Why?', science is concerned with the objective and impersonal, religion is concerned with the subjective and personal. There is some truth in these contrasts but, taken in isolation, they imply too stark a division between the two. 'How?' and 'Why?' are certainly different questions but if their answers are to make sense there must be some consonant relationship between them. If concerning some future action, a person answers the Why question by stating their intention to make a beautiful garden but answers the How question by saying that they are going to cover the ground with green concrete, then there is a perceived clash between the two responses, despite the alleged independence of the questions. The Christian doctrine of creation has certainly had the tone of its discussion modified by the scientific discovery that the universe did not spring into being ready-made a few thousand years ago.

Dialogue

Here there is a recognition that science and theology have things to say to each other about phenomena in which their interests overlap. Obvious examples of these boundary regimes are the history of the universe, the coming-to-be of life, the nature of the human person and the relationship between mind and body.

Integration

The aim here is more ambitious, for it encourages the unification of science and theology into a single discourse. An example would be the writings of Teilhard de Chardin which wove together biological evolution and spiritual development into a single account, culminating in Omega, which was envisaged as both the goal of physical process and the coming of the Cosmic Christ.

These last two categories – dialogue and integration – are the ones of interest in a study of the active interaction of science and theology. Polkinghorne has redescribed this intellectual meeting ground in terms of an alternative classification: consonance and integration.

Consonance

Science and theology retain their due autonomies in their acknowledged domains, but the statements they make must be capable of appropriate reconciliation with each other in overlap regions. In terms of the previous discussion, the answers to 'How?' and to 'Why?' must fit together without strain. It would be hard to harmonize the long, patient process of biological evolution with a theological notion of a God who habitually acted with instant and arbitrary power.

Assimilation

Here there is an attempt to achieve the maximum possible conceptual merging of science and theology. Neither is absorbed totally by the other (that would be to turn back to the picture of conflict, with a clear winner) but they are brought closely together. An assimilationist would be tempted to use evolutionary ideas to provide a clue to understanding the status of Jesus, seen as representing a 'new emergent', a further unfolding of human potentiality.

These taxonomic possibilities need testing in the light of further discussion of the actual interaction found to be taking place between scientific and theological thinking. This is a task to be tackled in the chapters that lie ahead.

Models, Metaphors and Symbols

Neither science nor theology can give plain, matter-of-fact accounts of the unseen realities (quarks; God) of which each needs to speak. Both also encounter situations too complex to be discussed without some degree of selective simplification. Thus science and theology must both make use of analogical resources in their reflective discussions. This chapter concludes with some discussion of the devices employed.

Models

In science, models are constructed by abstracting from a complex situation those features that are thought to be of greatest significance for the generation of the particular phenomena under study. Molecules are not tiny billiard balls, but the kinetic theory of gases can function successfully in those terms because its aim is to explain certain bulk features of gases (such as temperature and pressure) and these can be modelled adequately in this way. The same theory is incapable of explaining other features of gases, such as their behaviour in the presence of electrical discharges. The success of models, therefore, is always modest, depending upon the exploitation of partial similarities and not pretending to yield a completely valid representation of the entities being discussed. The purpose of models is limited explanation, not total description. As Barbour says, they are 'to be taken seriously but not literally'. Because of their restricted purpose, there is no perplexity in using a variety of seemingly contradictory models in order to understand a variety of different aspects of behaviour. When nuclear physicists are thinking about the scattering of protons by nuclei, they may use a 'cloudy crystal ball' model of the nucleus; when they are thinking of nuclear fission, they may use a 'liquid drop' model instead. No reconciliation between these two models is either possible or necessary. Only when science proposes a theory – that is a candidate for a verisimilitudinous description of a domain of physical reality – is it the case that it must insist on a single, consistent account.

Theology often has recourse to models. It may speak of God as stern Judge or merciful Father. The choice will depend upon the kind of divine encounter for which understanding is being sought. Once again, no claim of ontological adequacy arises for any model, and tension between two models is to be resolved by considering the differing experiences to which they apply (human repentance/divine acceptance in the case of the Judge/Father).

Metaphors

A metaphor is a literary device by which one speaks of one entity in terms of another. An often-discussed example is 'Man is wolf'. Involved here is no point-by-point comparison of human nature and wolf nature, with partial correspondences explaining a specified set of phenomena. Instead, there is a creative juxtaposition of the idea of man and the idea of wolf, resulting in a conjunction which has an unfettered power to illuminate both concepts in a way that cannot be fully articulated other than by the

23

metaphor itself, and that cannot be limited in its scope to a precise set of applications.

Peacocke quite often speaks of science as employing metaphor in its account of physical reality, but Polkinghorne denies this, claiming that, at most, science employs the plain comparisons of simile, much as in its use of models.

Theology can certainly take advantage of the open character of metaphor as an aid in its attempt to express experience of the Infinite in the language of the finite. However, there is another form of analogical device which appears particularly apt to the needs of theological expression.

Symbol

Symbols go beyond metaphors in two ways. First, they are not exclusively literary in character, for artefacts can also be the carriers of symbolic significance. Second, symbols enjoy a power to participate in the reality to which they are related. A country's flag sewn on an anorak in order to identify the wearer's nationality is simply acting as a signifier of that fact. However, the national flag, when flown from the mast of a public building of state or carried in parade by the armed forces of that country, is acting as a symbol of the nation and its history, for it evokes all the complexity, ambiguity and pride that go with these living realities. That is why the burning of a national flag is such a powerful action and the source of anger and pain to the citizens of the country thus slighted.

Symbols verge on the sacramental and their life-participating qualities make their use indispensable for theological expression. A particularly potent form of symbol is *myth*, understood as meaning a story expressing a truth too deep to be conveyed adequately in any more literal way (and certainly not understood in the modern debased sense that equates myth with untruth). The continuing power of ancient stories – such as Adam and Eve in the garden, or Noah and the flood – and the way in which they still grip the human imagination and stir the human heart make plain the role that myth must play in articulating theological insight.

2

The Scientific Picture of the World

The pace of advance in science quickens every year, with the result that most of modern scientific discovery has taken place in the twentieth century. The physical world, apparently so orderly and clear in our everyday encounter with it, is found to be fitful and cloudy at its subatomic roots. In the nineteenth century, scientists had realized that the Earth, and life on it, had been very different in the past, but in the twentieth century the whole universe has been found to have had a long developing history. Even the splendid insights of Newton into the nature of classical (everyday) mechanics have been found to be but a part of the story of macroscopic physical process. In addition to the robust, predictable systems he considered (like pendulums and planets), there is a multitude of exquisitely sensitive systems whose behaviour is intrinsically unpredictable because the slightest disturbance will totally change its character. These scientific advances have had their influence on the interaction between science and theology and we need to pay attention to them.

Quantum Theory

The first hint of quantum theory came in 1900 when Max Planck realized that a troublesome paradox in the behaviour of electromagnetic energy (technically, the form of the spectrum of black body radiation) could be removed in an empirically successful way if one assumed that radiation was emitted or absorbed in packets, which he called quanta. In 1905, Albert Einstein showed that the way in which a beam of light ejected electrons from metals (the photelectric effect) made it reasonable to suppose that these quanta persisted after emission (they were like bullets from a gun, rather than the drips from a tap which subsequently merge into a mass of fluid). The greatest revolution in physics since Newton was under way. It culminated in the brilliant, and independent, formulations of mature quantum theory, made in 1925 by Werner Heisenberg and

Erwin Schrödinger. Subsequently, the significance of their discoveries was further elucidated by Max Born and Paul Dirac, with Niels Bohr acting all the time as the father-philosopher figure of this new physics community.

When the dust had settled, two things were clear. At one level, the formal difference between classical physics (Newton) and quantum physics (Heisenberg and Schrödinger) was perfectly straightforward. At a deeper level, the interpretation of the new theory was murky, and it remains so.

Superposition

At the formal level, the distinction lies in quantum theory's 'super-position principle' (Dirac), which permits adding together physical states that classically are totally immiscible. The point at issue can be illustrated by a quintessential quantum experiment, the double slit. As shown in the figure, electrons (or some other quantum entity) are emitted from a source, S, and they impinge upon a screen in which there are two slits, A and B. Beyond this screen there is a detecting screen, D, which indicates when electrons impinge upon it. For definiteness, we could suppose D to be a large photographic plate on which each electron leaves a mark. The rate at which S emits electrons is adjusted to ensure that they arrive at D one at a time, with a discernible interval between successive impacts. As they do so, one can observe the electron marks accumulating one by one.

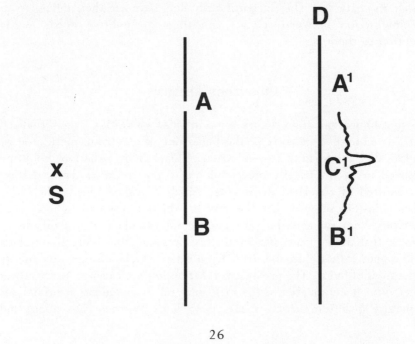

That is to say, the electrons are behaving like individual particles. When a large number of marks has been recorded, however, they are found to form a pattern of alternating intensity and diminishment, corresponding to the profile sketched in the figure. This 'interference pattern', as it is called, is absolutely characteristic of waves. It arises from the fact that at some points on D the wave from A and the wave from B will be in step (crest plus crest), giving reinforcement, and at other points they will be out of step (crest plus trough), giving cancellation. Thus the experiment clearly illustrates the well-known quantum paradox that the same entity can display both particle-like and wavelike properties. Since a particle is a little bullet and a wave is a spread out, flappy thing, such behaviour is totally unintelligible in classical terms.

One gets to the heart of the matter by asking the question, 'Which slit did the electron go through?' If the answer were A, then B would be irrelevant and it could have been closed up. But then the electron would have ended up near A^1, while, in fact, most of them end up in the middle at C^1. So the electron could not have gone through A. Standing the argument on its head shows that the electron could not have gone through B either. The only way out of the dilemma is to say that the indivisible electron went through both A and B! In other words, its state of motion is a mixture formed by adding together (going through A) and (going through B). Classically, this does not make sense, but quantum-mechanically this is precisely what the superposition principle permits. At once one encounters the mysterious everyday-unpicturability of the quantum world.

Strange as these results are, this much is well understood by physicists. The difficulties arise when we try to probe the matter further by adding to the experiment detecting devices designed to register whether the electron goes through slit A or slit B. Two things then happen. First, the altered experiment no longer gives an interference pattern at D. Second, sometimes the electron is found at A, sometimes at B; the two options occurring randomly but with equal probabilities.

The effect of these additional detecting devices that we added to the original double slit experiment draws our attention to the role of measurement in quantum mechanics. Instead of predicting a definite outcome, the theory only yields probabilities (50% at A, 50% at B). This random element has led most physicists to the belief that quantum theory is indeterminate and that quantum entities only possess definite properties (being at A, being at B) when one looks experimentally to see what these properties are. The making of such a measurement then yields a definite answer (A or B as the case may be). The unsolved interpretative problem in quantum theory is how the fitful quantum world yields in this way a definite answer each time it is subjected to experimental interrogation, despite the fact that the theory itself can only calculate probabilities for a range of possible results. This conundrum is called the measurement problem. It is also sometimes referred to as 'the collapse of the wavepacket'. If the electron is found at A, then only the A part of the original wave is now present; the superposition has been reduced to a single term. In other words, the wave from B has 'collapsed' or disappeared. It is this discontinuous change that abolishes the interference pattern centred on C^1, replacing it with a tighter pattern centred on A^1.

Measurement

No agreed or wholly satisfactory answer providing a solution to the measurement problem has yet been forthcoming. The following are the principal approaches that have been tried.

The original response was given by Niels Bohr and it is usually called the *Copenhagen interpretation*. Measurement is an intervention by the everyday (classical) world into the quantum world, producing a clear record in the classical measuring apparatus of a property of the quantum system under observation. Bohr essentially simply stated that this power of determination is a property that classical measuring apparatus is found to possess. There are quantum entities and there are measuring devices; put the two together and you get a result.

The trouble is that this is a dualist picture of the physical world (entity + apparatus), which simply will not do. The measuring apparatus is itself composed of quantum constituents. There are not two kinds of physical stuff around, but only one. At the very least, one needs a theory to explain why large complex systems (apparatus), though made out of indeterministic constituents, are able to play this determining role. There are some clues that might seem hopeful which can be found in the behaviour of complex systems. These systems are irreversible (that is to say they have a 'before' and 'after'; see p. 45), a property they share with measurement (afterwards one knows what one did not know beforehand). Yet so far a properly formulated modern version of the Copenhagen interpretation has not been worked out in detail.

Every experiment of which we know the result has been linked with a *conscious human mind*. Perhaps it is consciousness, that mysterious interface between matter and mind, that plays the determining role. This approach is really an attempt to link one mystery (measurement) with another mystery (consciousness). It faces a number of difficulties. Did no quantum process ever have a definite outcome till, late in cosmic history, minds came upon the scene? If the print-out from a computerized experiment is put away unseen in a drawer, is there no definite imprint on the paper until someone opens that drawer, many months later, and looks at it? Whose consciousness can do it, anyway? This latter point is illustrated by the poignant tale of Schrödinger's cat. The unfortunate animal is incarcerated in a box with a radioactive source which has a 50–50 probability of decaying in the next hour. If it does so, the decay will trigger the release of poison gas that will instantaneously kill the cat. At the end of the hour, and before anyone looks into the box, is the cat an even superposition of (alive) and (dead), or can its consciousness collapse the wavepacket? It seems hard to believe that the cat will not be aware of its own demise. But where do we stop? Can worms do it?

The most bizarre proposal is called the *many-worlds interpretation*. The apparent experimental verification of a particular outcome represents a discontinuous selection of a single one of a number of possibilities (A rather than B). Within the actual formalism of quantum theory (technically, the Schrödinger equation) there is no expression of this supposed discontinuity. The collapse of the wavepacket is imposed upon the theory from without.

Some physicists will have none of this. In their opinion, all that can happen does happen. It is a mere trick of our human perspective that we think that only one possibility has been realized. In their view, at each act of quantum measurement the world divides into a series of parallel worlds, in each of which one of the possible outcomes actually occurs. There is a world in which Schrödinger's cat lives and there is a world in which Schrödinger's cat dies. I may believe that I see a living animal but there is a clone of me in a parallel world (with whom I cannot communicate) who sees a dead one. Since quantum measurements are taking place all the time, the proposal is one of staggering prodigality. It has only commended itself to a narrow group of physicists. They are the quantum cosmologists, boldly endeavouring to apply quantum theory to the whole universe. In that case, there is no room left over for large measuring apparatus or even conscious observers. *Faute de mieux* we are left with the many-worlds interpretation. It is by no means clear, however, that quantum cosmology is a feasible proposition. If we do not understand how the microscopic quantum world relates to the macroscopic world of everyday experience, one might suppose that there would be even greater difficulties in its conjectured application to the cosmos.

The final proposal amounts to saying that there is, in fact, *no problem*. Quantum particles are as straightforwardly objective as Newton would have wished. The apparent uncertainties of quantum theory are simply due to the fact that not all the causal agencies at work are accessible to us. Covert causes of this unseen kind are called 'hidden variables'. David Bohm was the first person to construct an empirically successful theory of this nature. Its experimental consequences are identical to those of conventional quantum mechanics. Bohm's theory has both (objective) particles and also a wave that encodes information about the environment and which 'guides' the motions of the particles, without being itself directly observable. The existence of this alternative interpretation shows that the claimed indeterminacies of quantum theory are not absolutely required to be present but they are a matter of metaphysical choice. A deterministic, but partly hidden, account is perfectly possible. Most physicists, however, incline to Bohr rather than Bohm. Those who make this choice reflectively, rather than simply acquiescing in a consensus, do so because they feel that Bohm's theory, though very instructive, is too contrived in its character to be fully persuasive. This choice is made on strictly non-empirical grounds, but that does not mean that it is not a rational scientific decision, since science involves more than mere empiricism.

The greatest paradox about quantum theory is that, though it has been used with great success for more than seventy years, such a fundamental aspect of its interpretation as the nature of measurement remains un-understood and a matter of dispute.

Other Properties

There are a number of other aspects of quantum theory that have metaphysical implications and which, therefore, require our attention:

The Uncertainty Principle. Heisenberg showed that the existence of quanta implied certain restrictions on how accurately one could measure simultaneously different properties of a quantum entity. In popular language, if you know where an electron is (position), you can't know what it's doing (momentum), and if you know what it's doing, you can't know where it is. These restrictions can be neatly formulated in simple rules and they arise from the fact that the existence of quanta sets a minimum level for the amount of energy exchanged in an interaction (it cannot be less than one quantum packet), with the consequent implication that there is an irreducible amount of uncontrollable disturbance generated when a measurement is made.

In its original form, Heisenberg's principle was epistemological, concerned with what we can know (measure). Very soon, he and almost all his colleagues were interpreting it ontologically, as a principle of indeterminacy rather than merely of ignorance. Heisenberg believed that quantum entities do not possess precise positions and momenta but only potentialities for these properties, which then only become actual when this is forced by an act of measurement. The existence of Bohm's alternative, objective interpretation shows that this widely held view is not entailed by the physics but it is embraced by the physicists in an act of metaphysical choice. This decision corresponds to the realist strategy of seeking as close an alignment as possible between epistemology and ontology. In a phrase of Polkinghorne's, 'Epistemology models ontology'; what we can or cannot know is taken to be a reliable guide to what is the case.

Complementarity. Ask a quantum entity a particle-like question and you will get a particle-like answer; ask a wavelike question and you will get a wavelike answer. Bohr pointed out that, strange as this is, it involves no simple logical contradiction, since the apparently conflicting answers arise, in fact, from mutually exclusive experimental interrogations. They cannot both apply at the same time. (Technical note: Later, Dirac constructed quantum field theory which provides an explicit formalism possessing this property, so that physicists now understand the nature of wave/particle duality. It turns out to depend upon the superposition principle; a wavelike state contains an indefinite number of particles; see p. 26). Since one can measure exactly either position or momentum but not both, it is possible to describe the behaviour of quantum systems either in terms of their position or in terms of their momenta. These pairs of alternatives (wave/particle; position/momentum) represent a property of quantum theory that Bohr called 'complementarity', namely that contrasting accounts, each in principle complete in itself, can be given of the same set of phenomena.

Non-locality. In the 1930s, Einstein and two young collaborators, Boris Podolsky and Nathan Rosen, drew attention to a counter-intuitive property of quantum theory which had till then escaped notice. It implied a non-locality (togetherness-in-separation) in the theory so that, once two quantum entities have interacted with each other, they retain a power to influence each other, no matter how widely they subsequently might separate. If entity A stays in the laboratory and entity B goes 'beyond the Moon', a measurement on A will have an immediate consequence for the state of B. It is important to understand that this effect is causal and ontological and not merely epistemological.

There is nothing counter-intuitive in an increase of knowledge about A leading to an increase in knowledge about B. Suppose that there is a black ball and a white ball together in an urn, and that you take one in your closed fist and I take the other in my closed fist. If later I open my fist and find that I have the black ball, then I immediately know that you, perhaps now miles away, have the white one. There is no paradox involved, because you always had the white ball; all that has happened is that I am now aware that this is so.

In the EPR effect (as it is called), something much more profound is happening. Measuring different properties of A induces different consequences for B. These consequences are the results of actual changes in the state of B, brought about by the measurements on A. (One might have thought that such instantaneous effects would contradict relativity theory, but the latter only forbids the propagation of information faster than light and one can show that the EPR effect cannot be used to send messages.) Einstein thought that all this was so crazy that it showed that there must be something incomplete in quantum theory. However, John Bell formulated certain experimentally testable consequences of EPR effects (the Bell inequalities) and beautiful experiments conducted in the 1980s by Alain Aspect and his collaborators showed that non-locality is indeed a property of nature.

Metaphysical Insights

The discovery of quantum theory has enlarged the range of our imagination about the nature of physical process. This enhancement has its influence on metaphysical thinking. Some possible lessons include:

The physical world is full of surprises. Common-sense thinking, based on everyday experience, can only act as a partial guide. Reality is always liable to exceed our prior expectations. What is 'reasonable' cannot be decided by pure thought alone but only by looking for evidence of what actually is the case. No one could have guessed wave/particle duality beforehand. It needed the nudge of nature for its discovery.

Reality is not the same as naive objectivity. Physicists believe in the reality of electrons but they do not think that they are picturable in simple objective terms. Electrons possess the potentiality for position and momentum rather than their permanent actuality. Einstein's long battle against the mainstream interpretation of quantum theory, despite his having been the grandfather of the subject, was motivated by his passionate belief in the reality of the physical world and by his mistaken belief that this reality required a classically objective character for all phenomena. In the minds of contemporary scientists, the guarantee of reality is not objectivity but intelligibility – they believe in electrons because their existence makes sense of great swathes of physical experience.

Another important lesson to be drawn from quantum theory is that there is no universal epistemology. The quantum world must be known as it is, within the limits imposed by the uncertainty principle and not with the clarity of a Newtonian epistemology, if it is to be known at all.

Holism. The togetherness-in-separation manifested by the EPR effect runs counter to any notion of a naive reductionism, simply treating the whole as the separable sum of its individual parts. To our surprise, we find that the subatomic world is one that cannot properly be treated atomistically. The implications of this remarkable discovery still await their full exploration.

The near universal preference among physicists for Bohr over Bohm serves as a reminder of the importance of *non-empirical criteria in scientific theory choice*.

There are also some lessons which, though sometimes claimed to stem from quantum theory, are not actually to be derived from it:

It is not the case that quantum theory is so odd that after it 'anything goes'. Though the proposition is very seldom stated with such crudity, there is a style of thinking that may be called 'quantum hype'. It quickly and illegitimately elides from, say, EPR to the claim that telepathy is explained. (Since the effect cannot be used to convey information, that cannot be the case.) The notion of complementarity may possibly be of some analogical utility to theology when the latter considers some of its own perplexing dualities (such as the assertion of the human and divine natures of Christ) but it is not of itself an explanatory principle. One must remember that the physicists understand why complementarity works the way it does for rather specific reasons in quantum theory, but this does not license the unthinking application of the idea to other disciplines.

It is not the case that the quantum world is totally dissolving in its character, in a way analogous to the Eastern idea of the play of *maya*. Quantum theory has its particle-like characteristics as well as its more diffused wavelike characteristics. One of its early successes was to explain why atoms are

33

relatively stable (it requires a 'quantum leap' to change their state, while in classical physical physics such changes can occur gradually). Quantum processes are controlled by certain conservation laws (energy and momentum cannot just disappear), in the same way as in classical physics. Quantum theory is cloudy but not vacuous. Structure is present, exemplified by the symmetry principles that are the basis for all modern theories of elementary particles. These principles generate persisting patterns into which the constituents of nuclear matter are organized.

Exactly what one can say about the influence of the observer on reality depends upon which solution of the measurement problem is espoused. At one extreme, Bohm and, in a rather different way, the many-universes interpretation, are as free from overall observer influence as is classical physics itself. At the other extreme, the consciousness interpretation gives the observer a significant role, but only to the extent of inducing one of a limited range of permitted outcomes. At most, it seems best to say that quantum theory may give rise to the idea of observer-influenced reality, but to eschew altogether talk of observer-created reality.

Cosmology

In the 1920s, Edwin Hubble discovered that the universe is expanding, with the galaxies receding from each other with velocities proportional to their mutual separations. Retrojected into the past, this behaviour implied the familiar and famous big bang cosmology, asserting a cosmic origin (some fifteen billion years ago according to current estimates) when the universe as we know it appears to have burst forth from a singular state of infinite energy and density. The theory received impressive support from the discovery of the cosmic background radiation. This cold radio noise fills the whole universe and it is most naturally understood as a kind of cosmic fossil, a re-echoing whisper from a time when the universe was about half a million years old and it had just become sufficiently cool for radiation and matter to decouple from interaction with each other.

Quantum Cosmology

One can try to trace back cosmic history as close to the singular point of origin as possible. On the one hand, this task is simplified by the fact that the very early universe is almost uniform and structureless, and so it constitutes a very easy physical system to consider. On the other hand,

34

however, the task is complicated by the fact that the very high energies prevalent at that early period lead the cosmologist into considering realms of the behaviour of matter which are beyond our certain knowledge and, therefore, open only to conjecture. One can say that the period of the universe's history from a cosmic age of about a thousand millionth of a second to an age of some millions of years is one about which we can have considerable confidence that we understand the relevant physics. Significantly later than that, the universe begins to become more structurally complicated. Earlier than that, theories become increasingly more speculative and precarious. Peak uncertainty is reached at the cosmic age corresponding to the Planck time, 10^{-43} seconds. This is the epoch at which the universe would have been so small that quantum effects were important for cosmology. Since there is still no fully satisfactory reconciliation between quantum theory and general relativity (the modern theory of gravity and so the basis of all cosmological theorizing), the many discussions of quantum cosmology that are offered in the popular literature must be treated with a degree of caution. One should remember the remark made by a great Russian theoretical physicist, Lev Landau, that cosmologists are 'often in error but never in doubt'. Certain general features are, however, of sufficient possibility and significance to warrant some discussion.

Since the tendency of quantum theory is to fuzz things out, the proposal that this would happen to the initial singularity is plausible. The universe would then have a finite age but no precisely datable beginning. Also plausible is the suggestion that the very early universe, at an age of about 10^{-35} seconds, underwent a kind of 'boiling of space' (technically, a phase change) which greatly blew up its size in an incredibly short time. This hypothetical process has been given the name inflation, and it provides a natural explanation of certain general cosmic features, such as the near uniformity of large-scale matter distribution and the close balance between the effects of galactic expansion and gravitational attraction, which otherwise would be hard to understand.

The quantum vacuum is not an empty nothingness but an active medium full of fluctuating energy. It is not wholly inconceivable that our universe might have originated in a vacuum fluctuation grossly swollen by inflation. (Technical note: its long life would then require the cosmos to have virtually zero total energy, due to the positive energy of matter and motion being cancelled by the negative potential energy of gravity.) Equally, there can be no scientific certainty that the cosmos originated in this way.

None of these proposals has been worked out wholly satisfactorily, but they have the status of conjectures with varying degrees of plausibility and motivation. What theological significance they might have, if true, is something we shall have to consider in a later chapter when we consider the doctrine of creation.

The Anthropic Principle

We have noted that the smoothing action of inflation would produce a close balance between the expansive effect of the big bang, throwing the matter of the galaxies apart, and the cohesive effect of gravity, pulling matter together. The result was a universe which neither became rapidly very dilute nor quickly collapsed in upon itself again. Only such a balanced world could contain enough interaction between its constituents, and also enjoy a long enough continuing history of that interaction, to enable a fruitful development such as is represented by the coming-to-be of terrestrial life.

In the first three minutes of its existence, the whole universe was sufficiently energetic to be the arena of nuclear reactions. When cooling brought this period to an end, the gross nuclear structure of the cosmos was fixed, as it remains today, at three quarters hydrogen and one quarter helium. The abundance of hydrogen meant that when, after about a billion years, the action of gravity brought about the clumping of matter as it condensed into stars and galaxies, the steady supply of energy afforded by hydrogen-burning stars, like our Sun, was available to fuel the development of life. Another, anonymous, star played a vital role in enabling our eventual existence. The chemical raw materials of life (carbon, oxygen, etc.) can only be made in the nuclear furnaces of stellar interiors. A delicate chain of nuclear reactions turns the aboriginal hydrogen and helium into these heavier elements and permits some stars to end their lives in a supernova explosion, thereby scattering their nuclear material out into the surrounding space, where it can provide a suitable chemical environment on a second generation planet like the Earth.

Scientists understand the physics of these fertile processes pretty well. It turns out that they all depend, in different ways, on the forces of nature being precisely what they actually are in our universe. Very small changes in the quantities specifying the physical fabric of the world, such as the intrinsic strength of gravity or of electromagnetism, would have rendered cosmic history boring and sterile. In other words, a universe capable of evolving carbon-based life is a very particular universe indeed, 'finely tuned' in the character of its basic physical processes, one might say. This surprising insight is called the 'Anthropic Principle'. Not any old world is capable of producing *anthropoi*, beings of a complexity comparable to that of humankind.

This insight is reinforced by a consideration of terrestrial biological processes. The homeostatic mechanisms, which have kept the oxygen content of the Earth's atmosphere, its temperature and the salinity of the seas within tolerable limits, are also delicately balanced. The many remarkable properties of water seem essential if life is to be able to develop and they are consequences of the precise character of the structure of our world. Even the vast size of the observable universe – a hundred thousand million galaxies, each with a hundred thousand million stars – is necessary for the evolution of life on at least one planet. The process takes fifteen billion years and the cosmologists know that only a universe at least as big as ours could have lasted that long.

Although we only have direct scientific experience of one universe, scientists can use their imaginations to visit in thought other possible worlds that are 'nearby' ours, in the sense that they are similar to this universe but, for example, there are different intrinsic force strengths operating in them. The conclusion from such mental voyaging is that our universe represents a very tiny fertile patch in what is otherwise a desert area of possibility. For the development of fruitful complexity one needs: the right laws (neither so rigid that nothing really new can happen nor so floppy that only chaos can ensue – quantum mechanics seems ideal from this point of view); the right kind of constituents (a universe consisting just of electrons and photons would not have a rich enough potential for varied structure); the right force strengths (e.g. nuclear forces able to generate the elements inside stars); and the right circumstances (e.g. a big enough universe). The Anthropic Principle is widely accepted in this scientific sense. There is greater variety of opinion about what wider significance might or might not be attached to that conclusion.

The so-called Weak Anthropic Principle simply states that our presence in the universe implies that its nature must be consistent with its having evolved carbon-based life. For example, it is no accident that our universe is fifteen billion years old; a ten-billion-year universe would not have had time to produce *anthropoi*. This form of the Principle states the obvious but it fails to encapsulate the remarkable character of the tight constraints that are necessary to ensure that this is so. On the other hand, the Strong Anthropic Principle, which alleges that the universe must be capable of evolving life, does not have the character of a scientific principle, for its teleological nature surely means that it has to look beyond science to some other ground of belief in order to provide an explanation.

A philosopher who has considered these issues is John Leslie. He tells the following parable: You are about to be executed. You are tied to the stake, your eyes are bandaged and the rifles of ten highly trained marksmen are levelled at your chest. The officer gives the order to fire and the shots ring out . . . You find you have survived! What do you do? Do you just walk away, saying, 'That was a close one!' Of course not. So remarkable an occurrence demands an explanation. Leslie says that there are only two possible rational accounts of how you came to be so fortunate. One is that many, many executions are taking place today. Even the best of marksmen occasionally miss and you happen to be in the one where they all miss. The other explanation is that more was happening than you were aware of. The marksmen were on your side and they missed by design.

One sees how this story translates into thinking about the Anthropic Principle. Invoking its weak form would be equivalent simply to shrugging one's shoulders at having survived. Yet so remarkable an event surely demands an adequate explanation. It is important to recognize that what drives the search for a metascientific understanding of the Anthropic Principle is not just the apparently large odds against a very particular set of physical laws occurring among the vast portfolio of conceivable possibilities, but the combination of that improbable specificity with a deep significance. Any particular arrangement of white pebbles on green grass is hugely unlikely, because there are so many possibilities for the way in which they could be strewn around. We only get interested in a specific pattern if it carries heightened meaning for us, such as spelling out SOS.

The two explanations offered by Leslie translate in anthropic terms either into a many universes account or an account in terms of the will of a Creator. On the one hand, if there are many, many different universes, each with is own physical laws and circumstances, then it might be, by chance, that in one of them the conditions were just right for the evolution of carbon-based life. That is the universe in which we live because we could appear in the history of no other. On the other hand, there may be just one universe, whose finely tuned physical fabric represents the fertile endowment provided by the Creator whose will is that its history should be productive of life.

Both of these proposals are metaphysical in character. They go beyond what unaided science can aspire to tell us. The many universes account is sometimes presented as if it were purely scientific, but in fact a sufficient portfolio of different universes could only be generated by speculative processes that go well beyond what sober science can honestly endorse. An example of such a metascientific idea would be the hypothesis that the universe eternally oscillates, the big bang subsequent on each big crunch producing a world with totally different physical laws. (Many-universes quantum theory, even if true, would not be adequate since its multiple worlds differ only in the outcomes of quantum processes and not in basic physical laws.) The metaphysical proposal of the existence of a Creator will be given further consideration in Chapter 4.

Evolution: Chance and Necessity

The universe started extremely simple, but in the course of its fifteen-billion-year history there has been generated a rich profusion of complex structure. This has happened by evolutionary process, often characterized as involving both chance and necessity. By 'chance' is meant historical contingency, that this happens rather than that. By 'necessity' is meant the lawful regularity of physical process. The fruitful history of an evolving cosmos has involved an interplay between these two aspects of process, not only in biological evolution on Earth but also in the physical development of the universe itself.

The particular pattern of slight inequalities existing in the almost uniform distribution of matter in the early universe was enhanced by the lawful action of gravity to produce the particular pattern of condensed galaxies that we observe today. A different set of initial inequalities would have resulted in a different detailed galactic distribution. The specific structure we see is therefore present 'by chance' (it could easily have been different) but that there are galaxies seems no accident (that is what gravity brings about in an almost uniform world of not too dilute matter). Similarly, by chance, genetic mutations turn the stream of life in one direction rather than another, while the comparatively accurate transmission of genetic information across the generations preserves the integrity of species, enabling them in the longer term to participate in the process of natural selection operating in a lawfully regular environment.

A number of comments can be made about the nature of this universal evolutionary process:

Both chance and necessity are indispensable partners in the fruitful history of the universe. A purely contingent world would be too haphazard to be fertile; a purely necessitarian world would be too rigid to be fertile.

The role of chance does not turn evolution into a cosmic lottery; its presence need not imply the unfolding of an inane history. Rather, its meaning is that, since only a fraction of possible happenings can become actual happenings, what proves to be the case is a contingent selection from the total conceivable range of possibility. The shuffling actions of chance can be understood as a way of exploring and realizing some part of the potency contained in the physical fabric of the world.

Not only is necessity the indispensable partner of chance, but the insights of the Anthropic Principle remind us that this necessity *has to take a very specific form in a fruitful universe.* The evolutionary explorations of chance would be futile if the character of physical law were not tuned to anthropic potentiality. Conversely, given an anthropic world, the development within it of some kind of carbon-based life is a natural possibility. It is surely contingent that there are giraffes and that their average neck length has a certain value, but that there are now living beings somewhere in the universe is a possibility that seems to have been built into its future from the very start. There is unresolved disagreement among the experts concerning how readily this possibility could be realized. Some (Eigen, de Duve) believe that any planet with the right conditions of temperature, radiation, chemical composition, etc. may be expected to give rise to its own form of life. Others (Francis Crick) find it hard to understand how the appearances of life can have happened even once. While we remain ignorant of the biochemical pathways by which life has actually evolved here on Earth, these disputes cannot be settled. The unambiguous discovery that life independently arose on Mars, or elsewhere in the galaxy, would provide a vindication of those who feel that the universe is seeded with life.

Chaos and Complexity Theory

For many generations, scientists who learned about the classical mechanics of Newton did so by studying simple systems, such as a steadily ticking pendulum or a ceaselessly revolving planet. These dynamical systems are robust – a slight disturbance induces only a slight variation in the way in which they behave. Their behaviour is predictable and controllable – in a word, it is mechanical. It was long assumed that this was the typical classical behaviour, so that the whole Newtonian world was thought to be unproblematically clockwork in its character. In the twentieth century, and most clearly in the last forty years, it has been realized that this is by no means the case.

There are many classical systems that are exquisitely sensitive to the small details of their circumstances. In consequence, the least disturbance will totally change the way in which they behave. In a phrase going back to Karl Popper, they are 'clouds rather than clocks'. A picturesque way to symbolize this situation is to refer to the butterfly effect: the Earth's weather systems are so sensitive to small disturbances that a butterfly, stirring the air with its wings in the African jungle today, could have consequences that grew so rapidly (exponentiated) that they would bring about storms over London or New York in about three weeks' time!

Chaos Theory

The account of these hypersensitive systems has been given the name of 'chaos theory'. The nomenclature is unfortunate (but by now irreversible) since, although their unpredictable character generates future behaviour that appears haphazard, it turns out that this is not totally so but the range of future possibilities is contained within the limits of what is called a 'strange attractor'. There is both order and disorder in the behaviour of a chaotic system.

Mathematically, the equations describing a chaotic system have the properties of being reflexive (effects feed back upon their causes) and non-linear (doubling the cause does not just double the effect but it produces something quite different). The geometrical character of their solutions does not correspond to the continuous smooth curves characteristic of robust systems, but to the jagged geometry of fractals (saw teeth made out of saw teeth made out of saw teeth ... an unending proliferation of structure, similar on every scale of distance on which it is surveyed). Newton invented the calculus to deal with continuous smooth variation. It has turned out that the description of the physical world demands an enhancement of our mathematical imaginations beyond that orderly possibility. The general form that this new mathematics should take has not yet been worked out. Its study is still at the 'natural history' stage of looking at lots of particular examples provided by the investigation of computational models. Chaos is currently a computer-driven subject.

It is often called 'deterministic chaos', since the equations from which its models are derived are all perfectly well-behaved deterministic equations. If one knew exactly the initial conditions (a precise starting point), then a unique future history would follow. However the slightest uncertainty about these initial conditions (a slightly fuzzy starting point) will soon produce large uncertainty about future consequences, as the small variations grow exponentially and dominate behaviour.

As an example, consider the air in a room. The air molecules collide with each other in ways that are adequately modelled for present purposes by treating them as if they were miniature billiard balls. In 10^{-10} seconds, each molecule has had about 50 collisions with its neighbours. One then asks the question, How accurately must circumstances be known initially if one is to calculate with tolerable accuracy 10^{-10}

seconds later whether a particular molecule is moving towards or away from the back wall? A billiard ball collision is a perfectly determined event (Newton himself first worked out the theory), but a little error in the details of how two balls collide results in a much greater consequence for the directions in which they separate, as pool and snooker players know full well. Over 50 collisions these effects exponentiate, with the consequence that a serious error in prediction will be made in our problem if one has failed to take into account the effect of an electron (the smallest particle of matter) on the other side of the observable universe (about as far away as you can get) interacting with the air in the room through its gravitational effect (the weakest of the forces of nature). This astonishing conclusion not only illustrates the unpredictability of chaotic systems but also it shows that their vulnerability to circumstance means that they have to be considered in the context of their total environment. Even so simple a system as air molecules, in so short a time as 10^{-10} seconds, requires literally universal knowledge for a complete description.

Various metaphysical interpretations have been offered of chaos theory's combination of apparently deterministic equations and apparently unpredictable behaviour:

Determinism. The most common proposal accepts the equations at face value and draws the conclusion that complicated and apparently haphazard behaviour may originate from an underlying simplicity and determinism. There is a degree of epistemological pessimism implied by this stance, since it then seems impossible to tell the genuinely random from the apparently random.

Openness. An alternative proposal, put forward by Polkinghorne, is to give primacy in interpretation to the observed behaviour. Just as Hesenberg's uncertainty principle led most physicists to believe in quantum indeterminacy, so it is suggested that chaos theory should encourage belief in a more subtle and supple physical reality than the clockwork world of Newton. (Clouds are real and not just wobbly clocks.)

Polkinghorne claims that this is a natural step for a critical realist to take. Since something brings about the future, this proposal would imply that there are causal principles at work additional to the effects of energy interchange between constituents. Since paths through a strange attractor differ in patterns of behaviour rather than in energy, these new principles would relate to the structure of future behaviour rather than to energy input. Since chaotic systems are unisolatable, the new causal principles would have an holistic character. The term 'active information' has been coined to describe this new kind of causality ('active' because of its causal efficacy; 'information' because it concerns the formation of patterns of behaviour). The deterministic equations, from which the mathematical investigations began, are then regarded physically as approximations valid only in the specific circumstance that the effect of the environment on the system could satisfactorily be neglected. This latter condition restricts application to very particular regimes, but precisely to those in which experimental investigations are actually designed to take place. It is only the existence of these special isolatable circumstances that makes empirical science possible, for if one had to know everything before one knew anything, no scientific progress could be made. There is, therefore, no conflict with experimental knowledge in supposing the well-tested equations of Newtonian dynamics to be approximations in this sense.

It might be hoped that further enlightenment would result from synthesizing chaotic dynamics with quantum theory. After all, the behaviour of chaotic systems soon comes to seem to depend upon a fineness of detail at the level of Heisenberg uncertainty and below. However, great technical difficulties have been encountered in understanding the chaos/quantum interface and the matter is currently unresolved.

Order out of Chaos

Additional enhancement of our scientific imagination has resulted from the study by Ilya Prigogine and his colleagues of the behaviour of dissipative systems far from equilibrium. These are systems that are being maintained by an inflow of energy from their environment. The second law of thermodynamics, which specifies that the entropy (measurement of disorder) of an isolated system cannot decrease, does not apply in this case. Because of their interaction with their environment, dissipative systems can export their entropy, thus enabling them to generate and maintain a highly orderly internal pattern. The formation of this pattern can come about sponaneously through the enhancement of small fluctuations.

A simple example is provided by Bénard flow in fluids. A liquid is contained between two horizontal plates, the lower of which is maintained at a higher temperature than the upper. When the temperature difference between the two plates is sufficiently great, heat transfer takes place by convective bulk motion of the hot fluid from the lower plate to the upper plate, together with the downward return flow of cooled fluid. It turns out that this motion is highly ordered, the convective movements

43

of the liquid being contained within hexagonal cells of a definite size. This spontaneously generated order involves the correlated motion of trillions of fluid molecules. Many examples are known of this 'order out of chaos' (to use Prigogine's phrase). Living systems maintain their highly complex order by being dissipative systems. (We breathe out entropy).

Complexity

The whole history of the universe, and particularly the history of biological life on Earth, has been characterized by the steady emergence of complexity. The story moves from an initial cosmos that was just a ball of expanding energy to a universe of stars and galaxies; then, on at least one planet, to replicating molecules, to cellular organisms, to multi-cellular life, to conscious life and to humankind. Although this has come about over billions of years, when one considers the degree of intricate structure generated, it all seems to have occurred with remarkable rapidity. The simple evolutionary interplay of chance and necessity has certainly been part of that story. Darwin told us something of great value about the history of life.

It is interesting, nevertheless, to ask whether there might not be more to tell scientifically. The spontaneous generation of order out of chaos, and the possibility of active information as a causal principle, encourage the thought that this might be so. Further encouragement has come from the study of neural net systems, linked arrays of centres that are capable of correlated influence upon each other. Again one encounters, in appropriate regimes, the spontaneous appearance of long-range structured patterns of very specific kinds. Stuart Kauffman has suggested that there may be certain types of order, exemplified frequently in biological systems, that result from a natural propensity for matter to organize in particular complex ways. In other words, the course of biological evolution, in Kauffman's opinion, may have been influenced not only by the fitness criterion of survival in a particular ecological niche, but also by intrinsic ordering principles that favour the emergence of specific kinds of structure. (A very simple physical example would be that in Bénard convection, an hexagonal pattern of cells is favoured over a square pattern.) These scientific suggestions are currently at a very preliminary stage of investigation, but it scarcely seems open-minded to write them off on the prior assumption that Darwinism should not be in need of any further scientific augmentation. On the contrary, there is the intriguing and exciting prospect of a better understanding of the great drive towards complexity that has characterized cosmic and terrestrial history.

Time

St Augustine said that he knew what time was until he came to think about it and then his perplexities began. Although temporal process is fundamental to scientific thinking, scientists have also displayed a good deal of puzzlement about what they can say about the nature of time.

Reversibility

If one were to film the collision of two billiard balls, the film would make equal sense whether it were run backwards or forwards. A process of this kind is called 'time reversible'; it has no intrinsic 'before' or 'after'. On the other hand, a film of a large number of billiard balls on a jiggling surface which ended with the balls all at rest in a perfect rectangular array, is clearly a film being run backwards, for it shows a transition from disorder to order that runs contrary to our experience, which is that order gives way to disorder, rather than the other way round. This latter intuition is an expression of the second law of thermodynamics, that in an isolated system entropy does not decrease. (The specification that the system is isolated is clearly essential since an external intervention could readily force the balls into an orderly array.) Despite the reversibility of the individual collisions, a system of many billiard balls displays irreversibility. It has a natural definition of before and after. It is not the case that it is absolutely impossible for the balls to end up in an orderly array, but it is hugely improbable that they should do so, since this would require an extremely fine coordination between their individual motions. There are very few ways of being orderly and very many ways of being disorderly. Disorder always wins by an enormous margin.

These billiard ball lessons apply to the physical world in general. With one tiny exception (important in the very early universe but negligible now), the fundamental law of physics are time reversible. Irreversibility is an emergent property of large, complex systems. It is linked with the thermodynamic tendency to increasing entropy.

The Arrow of Time

The transition from 'before' to 'after' defines a direction for what may be called 'the arrow of time'. In fact, there are a number of definitions that define logically distinct arrows:

The thermodynamic arrow. This points in the direction of increasing entropy. (Technical note: there are some perplexities and disputed points about the application of thermodynamics to the whole universe. They arise from consideration of the exact sense in which it might be said to be an isolated system and from some subtleties in the thermodynamic properties of large-scale gravitating systems.)

The arrow of complexification. This points from the almost structureless early universe to the highly structured contemporary world. Our earlier discussion of dissipative systems shows that there is no necessary clash between the emergence of local structure and the second law of thermodynamics.

The cosmic arrow. This points in the time direction in which the universe is expanding.

The psychological arrow. This is defined by the human experience of the moving present, continually taking us 'forward' in time, turning an unknown future into a remembered past.

All these arrows point in the same temporal direction. This mutual alignment is not well understood.

Simultaneity

Newton assumed a steadily flowing absolute time to which all observers had unproblematic access. Einstein's great insight was that a more instrumental approach was needed to the measurement of time. An observer can only synchronize his clock with that of another observer if the two can send messages to each other and know the time elapsed in the sending. (The observer receives the message, 'It is now twelve o'clock' and knows that it took five minutes to get to him, so he sets his clock at 12.05.) Part of the fundamental basis of special relativity are the requirements, first, that no message can be transmitted faster than the velocity of light and second, that the velocity of light is the same for all observers. An immediate consequence of this is that the judgement of the simultaneity of distant events depends upon the state of motion of the observer making it. To see that this is so, consider the following simple example.

A lamp is located at the midpoint of a spaceship which is travelling at a velocity relative to a nearby planet that is an appreciable fraction of the velocity of light. The bow and stern of the ship are labelled A and B, respectively. As the midpoint passes an observer O on the planet, the light flashes. Another observer, O^1, located on the spaceship, will judge that the flash reaches A and B simultaneously, for it has the same distance to travel, namely half the length of the ship. The observer O, however, makes a different judgement. The light flash travels at the same velocity for O as it does for O^1 but for O it has less distance to travel to reach B, since the motion of the ship while the light is in transit will bring B nearer to O, shortening the journey time. Similarly, for O, the light's journey time to A is lengthened. Thus, for O the two arrivals are not simultaneous. There is, therefore, no absolute simultaneity; observers on the ship and the planet judge it differently.

The Block Universe

The dynamical equations of fundamental physics describe how properties change with a temporal parameter, t, but they contain no identifiable reference to the present moment. 'Now' is not a part of the current scientific description of the world, however fundamental it seems in our experience of that world. This has led some philosophors and physicists to suggest that all events, whatever their spatial location or temporal dating, are all equally real, all equally existent. The fundamental entity would then be the whole space-time continuum – a great chunk of frozen history, one might say. This claimed atemporal reality is called 'the block universe'. Its events have a relative temporal ordering (before and after), but no separation into past and future resulting from the motion of the dividing present moment. On this view, our impression that the past is known and the future unknown is a trick of human psychological perspective.

It is, of course, equally possible to note science's inability to incorporate the concept of 'now' and to interpret it as indicating the incompleteness of a description of reality in terms of contemporary physical theory alone. The block universe would then be regarded as an unjustified attempt at metaphysical imperialism on the part of physics.

Appeal is sometimes made to special relativity to underpin the concept of the block universe. Different observers construct different planes of simultaneity in space-time (they slice it up differently with their different versions of the temporal status of distant events). None can claim to be privileged, more real than any other, so all must be equally real. Adding them together, it is claimed, then produces the atemporal reality of space-time as a whole. On reflection, however, the argument is found to be flawed. Any observer's account of simultaneous distant events is always a retrospective construction, since the observer cannot be aware of such events until a signal is received from them, taking time to travel. By then the events are unambiguously past (technically, in the observer's backward lightcone). Thus the argument fails to achieve its purpose, for it carries no implication of the atemporal reality of the future.

Of course, if there is a genuine present moment, it must correspond to a special definition of time, selected from among the range of physically conceivable choices. As far as the physics of special relativity is concerned, that special choice would have to be hidden (physically indiscernible), but that only causes difficulties if one takes the material reductionist view that physics by itself should be capable of describing with total adequacy all that happens.

Logically, the reality of the block universe is distinct from the question of what causal relationships there might be between space-time events. There is no logical necessity for a block universe to be a deterministic universe. Nevertheless, there is some alogical linkage between the two concepts. On the one hand, in a deterministic universe, total knowledge of the present would enable total prediction of the future and total retrodiction of the past (as Laplace pointed out two centuries ago), so that in that sense it would be quite natural to accord past, present and future equal ontological status in this case. On the other hand, an open universe with a variety of causal principles at work, including the choices of free agents, is naturally conceived of as a world of true becoming in which the reality of a moving present would be expected to be accommodated, rather than a world of static atemporality.

3

Humanity

A most obvious and very important point of intersection between science and theology lies in the accounts they give of human nature. Men and women are a part of the physical world but they are distinguished from other entities in that world by their possession of self-consciousness and (a theologian would add) by their openness to encounter with divine reality. Physics, biology, anatomy and physiology, psychology, sociology and theology are all disciplines that will have something to say about the nature of humanity.

Physics will give an account of the basic properties of the constituents of our bodies, ultimately the quarks, gluons and electrons out of which the whole world, including ourselves, seems to be made. Biology will give an account of humanity's evolutionary emergence through the line of its hominid precursors, which links it to the rest of the animal kingdom. Both the distinctiveness of the human genome and also its considerable overlap with that of the higher apes will be among the biological data to be considered. Anatomy and physiology will give an account of the delicate web of structure and process that forms a living human body. Of particular concern will be neurophysiology's account of the intricate operations of the 10^{11} neurons in the human brain, with their 10^{14} interconnections, constituting far and away the most complex physical system known to us.

Psychology will offer a variety of accounts of human mental experiences, such as perception, memory and intellection. Sociology will set the individual human being within the network of relationships and the interplay of expectation and opportunity afforded by participation in a structured community. It will endeavour to assess the degree to which self-understanding and self-identity are constituted by the surrounding culture.

Theology will give an account of human religious experience, a varied but virtually universal phenomenon at all times and in all places, with the contemporary agnosticism and atheism of the Western world a decided anomaly in historical and geographical terms. The Christian theologian

49

will wish to speak of human sinfulness, understood in terms of an alienation from the God who is the ground of our being, and of Jesus Christ, both as the bringer of salvation to humanity through reconciliation to God and as the perfect archetype of what it means to be truly human.

Reductionism and Holism

The rich texture of human life is capable of being described in this varied and multi-layered fashion. A critical question, whose answer is much disputed, is what is the nature of the relationship between these different accounts. Are they all equally valid, each to be taken with the same seriousness and together forming a total picture through their consonant and complementary combination? Or does one level constitute the fundamental description of human ontology, with the others simply functioning as convenient manners of speaking about effects which actually are no more than derivatives from that one basic account?

Those who take the former view are called holists – for them humanity is an integrated package of rich complexity that must be considered in its many-layered entirety. The opposite of holism is some kind of reductionism, but it is important to recognize that this term is used in two broad and quite distinct ways, only one of which is a true contrary to an holistic view:

Constituent Reductionism

This simply asserts that when wholes are taken apart, then a limited range of constituent entities will be found among the resultant bits and pieces. For example, the statement made earlier, that the world seems to be made of quarks, gluons and electrons, would be a reductionist claim in this sense. If a human being were decomposed into constituents, that would be what would remain – there would be no extra life-giving ingredient left over, an *élan vital* or spark of life, distinguishing animate matter from inanimate matter. This is a widely held view, not least because it seems consonant with the history of the universe as told by science, continuously linking the quark soup that was the universe when it was 10^{-10} seconds old with the universe today, the home of life. It constitutes the weakest form of reductive understanding and it by no means implies that human beings are nothing but quarks, gluons and electrons, for the hypothetical decomposition would also have destroyed the man or woman subjected to it. Those who hold a view contrary to constituent reductionism are often called 'vitalists', for they suppose an additional vital element is required to turn inert matter into living being.

Process Reductionism

This much stronger claim asserts that higher level languages (such as those of biology or psychology) are just convenient manners of speaking about complicated happenings that actually are totally generated by the operation of the lower level physical laws and processes. For manageability, these higher level languages are indispensable, but they do not correspond to a fundamental element of reality. In principle, if not in actual practice, a complete account of human nature could be given in terms of the reduced description.

A well-worn but useful example from within physics itself is provided by the relationship btween thermodynamics (higher level) and the kinetic theory of gases (lower level). All that is happening in a gas is the collision of molecules, taking place according to the appropriate constituent laws. With, say, 10^{23} molecules involved, it is impossible to talk in individual molecular terms. A thermodynamic quantity like temperature, understood as directly related to the average molecular kinetic energy of the gas, is a necessary shorthand, describing a significant property of the aggregate of molecules. But that is all that temperature is; it is nothing but mean kinetic energy.

A process reductionist will make the same claim for all holistic properties including, in the human case, mental experiences, regarded as a direct summation of molecular processes in the brain. Many of those who hold the contrary view may be called 'contextualists', for they believe that the nature of individual processes depends upon the overall context in which they are taking place. Another way of expressing an anti-reductionist belief is to assert that there is 'top-down' influence of the whole upon its constituent parts, as well as the 'bottom-up' influence of the parts upon the whole.

There is a position, apparently intermediate between reductionism and a wholehearted contextualism, which is espoused by many writers and might be called 'conceptual emergentism'. Returning to the example of a gas, there is indeed no more than the ordinary intermolecular processes taking place, but on the other hand there can be no idea of temperature which is applicable to a small number of molecules. In this sense, the concept of temperature is irreducible, for it cannot be expressed in separate molecular terms. The attraction of this stance lies in its apparent ability to acknowledge elements of holism, corresponding to the way in which we actually talk about complex systems, without questioning the

51

universal applicability of the microscopic laws of physics. However, it is not really clear that this is more than reductionism veiled behind a mask of complexity (see the discussion of emergentism in the subsection on physicalism below).

Holists face the problem of how the different levels of description can be reconciled consistently with each other; how the bottom-up constituent interactions allow room for the operation of additional top-down effects. Reductionists face the problem of how the experiences and behaviours described at the higher levels, arise as epiphenomena (superficial by-products) of the processes taking place at the level considered to be of sole fundamental significance. The controversial issues between the holists and the reductionists have been discussed for many centuries, with meagre progress towards a resolution. A number of basic strategies have been pursued by participants in the debate.

Physicalism

This reductionist strategy treats the basic stuff of the world as being matter as described by physics, with mental experience regarded as an emergent consequence of matter in complex organization, amounting to no more than an epiphenomenal ripple on the surface of intrinsically material reality. It is clear that there are emergent properties of this kind in nature. An H_2O molecule does not possess the property of wetness; that belongs to large aggregates of such molecules. The way that energy is distributed between these molecules is modified by their mutual interactions, producing an effect that physicists call 'surface tension' and which corresponds to the experience of wetness. Such an emergence is complicated to calculate but unproblematic in character; energy exchanges between constituents produce an overall energetic property of the whole. It is very far from clear, however, that this affords any analogy for the emergence of mental experience, for that appears to have a character totally different from anything related to energy exchanges between bits and pieces.

One might have expected elementary particle physicists, studying the smallest known constituents of matter, to have been in the forefront of physicalism, for their discipline is clearly the ultimate basis for describing the world as physics understands it. They are certainly constituent reductionists. However, we have already seen (pp. 31–2) that one of the surprising consequences of quantum theory is that it is not possible to describe the subatomic world atomistically. There is an inescapable togetherness-in-separation (non-locality) that modifies a constituent account and points one in a holistic direction. Contemporary physical reductionism finds most of its supporters elsewhere than in fundamental physics.

Currently, many of the strongest reductionist claims are being made by biologists, particularly those who work with molecules rather than with organisms. The level at which the claims are pitched seems to be influenced by the discipline practised by the claimant. Thus the geneticist Richard Dawkins, in so far as he perceives any significance in physical process, appears to locate it at the level of the 'selfish genes', 'propagating themselves' from generation to generation of plant and animal life. In a notorious phrase, he spoke of human beings as being 'genetic survival machines'.

The contemporary biological scene is reminiscent of the state of physics in the post-Newtonian generation of the mid-eighteenth century. Both subjects scored notable initial successes (universal gravity and the solar system; the helical structure of DNA and the molecular basis of genetics). Both insights were of a mechanical nature (it is easier to understand clocks than clouds and one starts with the most accessible phenomena). Both sets of adherents then went on to declare that their new discoveries supplied the basis for understanding practically everything (de la Mettrie and his book, *Man the Machine*; Crick and Dawkins and molecular reductionism). Physics has discovered that the world is more subtle, supple and interesting than its eighteenth-century practitioners had supposed it to be. It is difficult not to believe that biology will make a similar discovery in due time.

We shall return to the claims of physicalism when we consider consciousness in the next section.

Idealism

This polar opposite of physicalism reminds us that all our actual experience of reality is appropriated mentally. Our belief in the existence of the physical world is derived from the interpretation of our sense perceptions. It is then claimed that if there is a single fundamental level at which to discuss reality, it is surely that of the mind. The most celebrated proponent of this point of view was the eighteenth-century philosopher, Bishop George Berkeley.

The idealist strategy has never attracted a great deal of support in Western thinking. Bluff Dr Samuel Johnson did not logically refute Berkeley when he kicked a stone, but most people find it hard not to accept that we are inhabitants of a world of matter which continually impinges upon us. Mental reductionism has proved a less beguiling option that material reductionism.

Dualism

In modern Western thinking, the dominant strategy from the seventeenth century on to the beginning of the twentieth century was dualism – the belief that humans are composed of two distinct substances, the material and the mental. The intellectual patron saint of this point of view was René Descartes, who asserted the existence of both extended matter (located in space) and thinking mind (not thus localizable). This option has the attraction of frankly recognizing the different characters of the material and the mental, and the merit of not downplaying either. It is the heir of a tradition at least as old as Plato. Yet this point of view also presents very considerable difficulties. Today, dualists are in a minority.

The problem has always been to understand how the disjoint realms of the material and the mental could relate to each other so as to constitute the degree of unity we experience as human persons. How does my mental intention of raising my arm get translated into the physical action of its motion? Descartes' successors were driven to the rather desperate expedient of invoking God's direct action to synchronize events in the separate realms of the material and the mental. Today, the more we know about the effects of drugs and brain damage on mental processes, and the more we consider the apparently continuous history linking the world of humanity with the primeval era when the universe was a mindless energetic quark soup, the more difficult it becomes to accept dualism – the idea of 'the ghost in the machine', in Gilbert Ryle's wittily dismissive phrase. A further difficulty with dualism was that, in practice, it frequently succumbed to the temptation to exalt the mental at the expense of the material.

If the two aspects of reality are to be held in equal balance, it seems that it will have to be in some way more subtle than mere juxtaposition. Some very tentative attempts have been made to think along such lines.

Dual-Aspect Monism

This strategy assumes that there is just one sort of world 'stuff', one substance, but it occurs in different forms of organization that give rise to the material and mental poles of our experience. A physicist might draw an analogy with the solid, liquid and gaseous phases in which a single kind of matter can be encountered. Each phase displays very different characteristics but each is composed of the same underlying entity. (This analogy is only of limited utility, however, since the contrasting properties of the different phases of matter are all expressions of energetic behaviour, so that their emergences are relatively unproblematic. Something infinitely more subtle must be involved in the interrelationship of the material and mental phases.) Dual-aspect monism is compatible with the historical coming-to-be of the mental through the increasing complex-ification of the material, but it in no way subordinates the mental to the material, treating it as if it were merely an epiphenomenon. Rather, it seeks to assert an even-handedness between these two poles of the world's reality.

Such a theory would be very attractive. The great problem has been to see how one could articulate a bipolar account of this kind. Recourse to hopeful analogy has been one technique. Perhaps the most promising resource might be quantum theory's notion of complementarity (p. 31). After all, wave and particle seem about as contrasting and irreconcilable as mind and matter. In the subsequent discussion of consciousness we shall see what might be made of this idea.

Process Thought

Yet another strategy is to suppose that the mental has always been present, along with the material, but originally in an attenuated form. In the course of cosmic history, and particularly in the evolution of complex beings, the mental has become focused and manifest, but it has not emerged since it has been there from the beginning. This idea has found developed expression in process thought, based on the pioneering metaphysical proposals of the philosopher, A. N. Whitehead. He supposed that the basic elements of reality are not entities but discrete events ('actual occasions'). Each event is bipolar. It has a 'prehensive phase', in which it is influenced by all past events (and also by the 'lure' of divine persuasion), and a 'concrescent phase', in which one possible outcome is actually realized. What we think of as entities are, in fact, chains of events.

It is clear that the bipolarity of prehension and concrescence reflects, in a suggestive way, the bipolarity of the mental and the material. Of course, it is not claimed that atomic events correspond to conscious experience; that will only be so in those highly complex and integrated events whose summation will correspond to a living being. Therefore, defenders of process thinking deny that it is pan-psychic, preferring the description 'pan-experiential'. Yet they see a continuum of experience linking protons to persons and they deny that there is an essential difference between the two ends of that spectrum of being. The distinctions lie in matters of degree.

One of the difficulties about process ideas is the graininess that is asserted as being present in reality, understood as a collection of actual occasions. The world that science discerns does not have this character. There are discontinuities encountered in quantum physics, but they are associated with occasional acts of measurement and there is also considerable continuity, expressed, for example, by the smooth operation of the Schrödinger equation. Another problem is the latent psychic-like pole assumed to be present, if only to an infinitesimal degree, in atoms and the like. It is not an instantly persuasive concept.

Insolubility

Perhaps humanity's desire entirely to understand itself is an attempt to grasp knowledge that is, by its very natue, denied to us. We can understand the physical world because we transcend it through our powers of self-consciousness and rationality. It is not so clear that our own nature may not always prove to be a mystery to us. It could be that we can no more understand what it is that we are, than we can pull ourselves off the ground by tugging on our own bootstraps. The many logical paradoxes deriving from self-reference ('What I tell you is false') might be warning signs to be heeded. To comprehend the human it might be necessary to stand outside the human, but in fact there is no such Archimedean point available to us.

This intellectually pessimistic view represents a possibility that should be borne in mind. The only way to find out whether it is true or not seems to be to push the other attempts at understanding as far as they will go and then evaluate the success or failure that results. While insolubility remains an ultimate possibility, it should be the strategy of last resort rather than an initial assumption. One way of attempting to carry the discussion a little further is to consider what progress has been made in comprehending the distinctive human property of self-consciousness.

Consciousness

The most remarkable event known to us in cosmic history following the big bang is the coming-to-be of consciousness. In humanity the universe has become aware of itself. As Blaise Pascal said, human beings are 'thinking reeds', greater than all the stars because we know them and ourselves, and they know nothing at all.

We all experience awareness, but we have virtually no understanding of its origin. A smart tap on the head with a hammer will establish that there is a relationship between mind and brain, but what that relationship actually is remains a matter of unresolved dispute. There is a particular difficulty in thinking about consciousness, because its presence is constitutive of all our known experience. Without it, we would have no knowledge whatsoever. Introspection simply reveals the current object of consciousness — what we are thinking about now — but not consciousness itself, which is as invisible and vital as the air we breathe.

Philosophy of Mind

Two distinct strategies can be discerned in the writings of contemporary philosophers concerning the nature of mind. The difference arises from their contrasting attitudes to common-sense reports of mental experience. Such accounts — of perceiving a patch of pink, of believing that John is a reliable person, of feeling the pain of toothache, of being thirsty and wanting a drink — correspond to what most people would regard as the staple contents of the conscious life. One strategy does indeed treat these reports as trustworthy, in which case they are the basic phenomena whose understanding is being sought. On the other hand, the alternative strategy regards them as misapprehensions, equivalent to the common parlance that the Sun 'rises', while actually it is the Earth that encircles the Sun and not vice versa.

Those philosophers, such as John Searle, who accept common-sense reports, point out that, in general, everyday speech is to be taken seriously since it has been winnowed by everyday experience and if it were grossly in error, that would have imperilled human survival. Those who take the contrary view, such as Daniel Dennett or Patricia and Paul Churchland, dismiss common-sense reports as mere 'folk psychology', traditional manners of speaking about phenomena whose real character is very different. Philosophers of this cast of mind often turn to bizarre thought experiments as the source of their insight — asking whether you might not be a brain maintained by an Evil Scientist in a vat of chemicals and continuously stimulated to give the impression of embodied existence, or questioning what happens to a person when their brain is split in two by a Callous Brain Surgeon and the right and left hemispheres are transplanted into the conveniently available bodies of identical twins. To assume the feasibility of these grotesque transactions is already to have presupposed the answers to a number of questions about mind and brain. Many will regard it as safer to rely upon the nature of their own actual mental experience and its congruence with the reports of others.

Another celebrated philosophical (and theological) problem with a long and disputed history is the issue of human determinism or free will. We certainly have the impression that we choose what to do, even if the researches of psychologists into unconscious motivation suggest that our room for manoeuvre is more circumscribed than we ordinarily acknowledge. Yet do we really possess what philosophers call 'the freedom of indifference' (the genuine option of doing either A or B) or do our apparent desire and our action have a common origin in a deeper determined mechanism within our brains, so that we only suppose that we are making a genuine choice? On its own, science is not of great help to us here. Certainly, modern physics has discarded the picture of a world of clockwork, but the kind of randomness that quantum events display is a far cry from the voluntary agency of persons. The issue of free will is a metaphysical issue and its resolution calls for metaphysical decision. Many theologians will wish to treat as basic the human intuition of free and responsible moral choice. There is nothing in contemporary science to forbid their doing so.

In the opinion of many thinkers, human freedom is closely connected with human rationality. If we were deterministic beings, what would validate the claim that our utterance constituted rational discourse? Would not the sounds issuing from our mouths, or the marks we made on paper, be simply the actions of automata? All proponents of deterministic theories, whether social and economic (Marx), or sexual (Freud), or genetic (Dawkins and E. O. Wilson), need a covert disclaimer on their own behalf, excepting their own contribution from reductive dismissal.

It is time to look at some of these issues in more detail by considering certain particular proposals.

Functionalism

One of the most popular reductionist strategies for tackling the relationship between mind and brain is to suppose the essence of the matter to lie in the processing of information, turning the input of signals from the environment into output of motor activity of various kinds (including speech). The question is then being discussed in a purely functional way.

Those who adopt this stance often seek to express it in the physicalist terms of a computer model of the brain. They take encouragement from the fact that our neural architecture bears some resemblance to that of a computer, particularly one based on processing by parallel arrays, though the brain is immensely more complex, and especially possesses an immensely greater connectivity, then any currently constructed computer. The triumphalist claims of the protagonists of artificial intelligence, that 'thinking' machines are on the horizon of achievement, are held to reinforce this view. Notable proponents of a functional approach have been Dennett (who considers human mental processes to be the result of an anarchic struggle in which many parallel neural computers produce 'multiple drafts', one of which wins out) and Francis Crick (whose account is mainly concerned with an interesting description of what is known of the neurophysiology of visual perception). Despite Dennett's over-ambitious title (*Consciousness Explained*), neither author comes anywhere near giving a convincing account of the fundamental human experience of awareness. There are a number of other serious difficulties with this functional approach.

If the brain were a computer, one would have to ask the question of what had programmed it. The answer usually given is that evolutionary necessity has shaped the neural processes of the brain to conform to survival requirements. Of course, there must be some truth in this assertion. Yet, it is difficult to believe that it furnishes an adequate, total explanation of human mental abilities.

Our intellectual powers greatly exceed anything that could credibly be required by natural selection – for example, what survival value attaches to the human ability to comprehend the processes of the subatomic quantum world or the structure of cosmic space? To regard this great excess of rational power as just a happy accident, a collateral spin-off from some more mundane necessity, seems peculiarly lame. Similar difficulties attach to explaining other forms of human intuition.

Sociobiology's claim to account for ethical insights in terms of covert strategies for genetic survival has been unconvincing. The widely acknowledged duty of altruism – to risk personal harm for the greater good of another – goes beyond anything made intelligible simply in terms of kin altruism (saving my children because they carry some of my genes) or reciprocal altruism (I will help you because I expect you to help me on another occasion). Such calculations can scarcely be supposed, even in a veiled way, to enter into the motivation of a person who saves an unrelated stranger from a burning building at considerable risk to themselves.

While efficient information processing must be a help to survival, it is far from clear why this must involve conscious awareness. Indeed, the existence of a focal point of attention may divert a person from recognizing the existence of danger elsewhere. Hence the use of impersonal systems to supplement human awareness in monitoring the safety of potentially dangerous manufacturing processes.

Roger Penrose has revived *an argument from mathematical logic* which he believes shows that human thought transcends what is possible through the operation of a computer. An appeal is made to the work of the logician,

Kurt Gödel. He showed that any axiomatic system of sufficient complexity to contain arithmetic (that is, the integers, 1, 2, 3 . . .) always contains propositions that are statable within the system but not decidable within it. Such a system would correspond to a programme running on a universal computer, the so-called Turing machine. The proof of this fundamental and surprising result depends upon the construction of a statement (the Gödelian sentence) which the mathematician can see to be true but which is not provable within the logic of the system under consideration. Penrose believes that this shows that mathematical thinking exceeds computation. The claim has been hotly contested, but Penrose has sustained a robust defence of his position.

Another argument leading to a similar conclusion of the limited character of computer modelling is provided by *Searle's philosophical parable of the Chinese room*. You are seated in a closed office. Through a grill, people hand you pieces of paper on which some squiggles are written. You look up the corresponding set of squiggles in a big book with which you have been provided and copy out the set of squiggles next to them. These you pass out through another grill. You have no idea what is going on, but in fact the incoming squiggles are questions in Chinese and the outgoing squiggles are the appropriate answers in Chinese. Understanding is located neither in you (the computer processor), nor in the big book (the programme) but in the author who compiled the book (the programmer). Computers can handle syntax but not semantics; they can follow grammatical rules but they do not have access to meaning. Yet understanding is fundamental to thought. Once again, the claim has been hotly disputed, but Searle maintains a stout defence.

It is characteristic of computer programmes that they can be run on any apt form of hardware (silicon chips, or an ingenious arrangement of water pipes and sluices, or whatever). If humans are not 'computers made of meat', maybe there is something specific in the nature of the 'meat' that makes this so.

Emergence

A much more vague, but also more plausible, proposal is that consciousness is an emergent property of biological systems of a sufficient degree of complexity. This stance does not necessarily imply a physicalist position, though it is compatible with a refined physicalism such as that professed by Searle, who does not deny the validity of mental concepts but believes that the appearance of consciousness with the formation of increasingly complicated life forms is no more problematic that the appearances of wetness when large aggregations of H_2O molecules are formed. We have already had reason to question this assertion (pp. 51–2). Searle's stance, which one might call materialist but not eliminative (since mental concepts still have a role to play), fails to face the huge gap between physical talk of neural networks, however sophisticated such talk may become, and the simplest mental experience, say of seeing red. The two languages seem completely incommensurable in a way that is not the case for molecules and wetness (for which energy provides the common factor). Therefore, we return to considering an analogy which might afford some modest help.

Complementarity

Accounts of waves and particles seem equally to be incommensurable. Yet, not only do quantum entities display both sets of properties, but also (contrary to assertions one often finds in the philosophical literature) we do understand how that seeming paradox is resolved. The clue lies in Dirac's discovery of quantum field theory. Because a field is a spread-out entity, it possesses wavelike properties. When it is quantized, it also acquires the discrete countability, characteristic of quantum mechanics. For example, its energy comes in packets, whole numbers of quanta of various kinds, precisely corresponding to particle-like properties. Closer examination reveals how the trick is done. Because of the superposition principle (p. 26), it is possible for a quantum field to have states that are mixtures of the states corresponding to definite numbers of particles. (Classically, of course, this would be impossible. In a Newtonian world, one has precisely n particles present, neither more nor less. You can count them.) It is these states with an indefinite number of particles that turn out to correspond to states with wavelike properties (technically, with definite phases). In other words, it is the quantum indefiniteness ('fuzziness') that permits the coincidence of opposites represented by wave/particle duality.

If this tale has a wider moral, one might hope that a dual-aspect monism, a mind/matter theory, might be possible if it too incorporated within itself a degree of intrinsic indefiniteness. Of course, in our present state of knowledge this is just an analogical guess. We cannot see in detail how this might work, but in the discussion of consciousness no one has access to more than hand-waving discussion. Speculations along these lines have been given some degree of consideration.

A number of authors, adopting a number of distinct strategies, have supposed that quantum theory itself might provide the indefiniteness sought. One problem with this idea is that quantum effects normally operate on the atomic scale or less, while the brain looks like an immensely complicated integrated macroscopic system. In consequence, some have sought to identify microscopic subsystems which they claim play a significant role in neural process and which are also small enough to be susceptible to quantum effects. (One is reminded of Descartes' rash speculation that the pineal gland was the seat of the soul.) An example of this kind of conjecture is Penrose's belief that small intracellular structures called 'microtubules' are of great importance in the generation of mind. (In passing, one may note that contemporary dualists, such as Sir John Eccles, also make similar suggestions for what they believe might be the interface [the 'liaison brain'] by which mind acts on the matter of the brain.) An alternative to this microscopic strategy is to suppose that mind is somehow linked with the quantum state of the brain as a whole. This is a difficult notion since the whole cortex, for instance, looks like a classical entity. When it is kept under continuous observation in a patient who has been trepanned, this does not seem in any way to change or inhibit mental activity.

Another possibility would be to consider a role for macroscopic indefiniteness. This would require an ontological interpretation of chaos theory of the kind already discussed (pp. 42–3). The notions of causality through energetic interaction of constituents on the one hand, and of causality through the top-down effect of active information on the other, have about them something of the flavour of the material and the mental in a complementary relationship. There might be here a glimmer of how mind and brain relate to each other. Nevertheless, it is clear that today we are still far away from resolving our perplexities about the origin and nature of consciousness, despite its providing the basis of all our knowledge and experience.

The Self and the Soul

A primary human concept is that of the continuing self, linking golden-haired youth to snowy old age. (At least, that is so in traditional Western thinking; Eastern thought has more frequently considered the individual self to be an illusion from which release is to be sought. In this book we shall take the Western view.) One of the attractions of dualist thought is that it assigns to each human person a spiritual component, a soul, which acts as the carrier of the self, defining a unique human identity in this life and beyond it. Yet the tenor of the foregoing argument has been to reject dualism and to treat human beings as psychosomatic unities, 'animated bodies rather than incarnated souls', in a famous phrase. This was the way in which the ancient Hebrews seem to have conceived of humanity and a psychosomatic account of human nature is the dominant, but not exclusive, way of thinking to be found in the Bible. One of the few matters relating to humanity on which there is a substantial degree of contemporary agreement is that men and women are to be treated as unities and not as spiritual beings housed in fleshly bodies.

This does not imply eschewing all talk of the soul – that would be a grave difficulty for much of theology – but a redefinition of what the soul might mean. In essence, it must be 'the real me'. It is clear that this is not simply the material that happens to compose my body at some particular time. The atoms in each of us are continually being changed by eating and drinking, wear and tear. They cannot be the source of our experience of a continuing self but, rather, we may suppose that the self is composed of the immensely complex 'pattern' in which that matter is organized. It is beyond present human power to explicate exactly what are the characteristics of this pattern, what changes (as new memories are acquired, for instance) and what remains the same (defining the continuing life of a specific person). The rejection of a computer model of brain/mind implies that it would be totally inadequate to think of the soul as the super-programme running on the hardware of the body, but that impoverished analogy would at least point in helpful direction, however much it might require augmentation in order to correspond to the profound complexity of human nature.

As with all attempts to describe humanity, one soon reaches the hand-waving stage of the discussion. Yet the need simultaneously to acknowledge both psychosomatic unity and also the existence of a carrier of human identity is an insight that has had a long philosophical history. Aristotle spoke of the soul as the 'form' of the body; in other words, he too thought of the soul as pattern. This way of thinking was taken up by Thomas Aquinas, who rejected the Platonic dualism that had dominated Western Christian thinking since Augustine. Such a view is the most widespread account adopted in contemporary theological discussions.

The Fall

Finally, we must consider a distinctive Christian assertion about humanity: that we are a fallen race. From St Paul onwards, the story of Adam and Eve's disobedience and expulsion from Eden (Gen. 3) has played a significant role in Christian thinking, in rather striking contrast to its apparent lack of importance in Jewish tradition. There is a consensus among modern theologians that the third chapter of Genesis is not a literal account of a single disastrous primeval incident, but it is a myth (that is to say, not a falsehood but a truth conveyed in narrative form, because only story could carry the necessary depth of meaning).

The myth of the Fall can be understood as an ever-contemporary symbol of the human condition. There is a slantedness in human affairs that leads to the frustration of hope and the tarnishing of intention. It turns a country's liberator into its next tyrant and it finds common expression in the shabby compromises and betrayals of everyday life. Reinhold Niebuhr once said that original sin (the moral twistedness of men and women) was the only empirically verifiable Christian doctrine! One has only to look at the world, or within one's own heart, to find confirmation. Genesis 3 portrays this experience in the post-Eden life to which Adam and Eve are condemned and it diagnoses its origin in a chosen alienation of humanity from God. In Christian understanding, we are not autonomous beings whose fulfilment lies in going it alone and doing it 'my way'; we are heteronomous beings whose life is incomplete if we are not reconciled to the Creator who is the ground of our being. Such an understanding of the Fall, in terms of contemporary experience, seems realistic and easily understandable.

Problems arise, however, when one goes on to ask how this state of affairs arose, how God's allegedly good creation came to be morally marred. The traditional answer, powerfully formulated by Augustine, attributed it to a literal act of disobedience by our first ancestors and it also supposed that this led to disastrous consequences for a previously paradisal creation, bringing on to its scene death and frustration (the physical evils of disease and disaster). Such a view is clearly untenable today, considered as an historical account. Earthquakes, volcanoes, hurricanes, animal death – all antedate the appearance of humanity on Earth by hundreds of millions of years.

From early times, there was a minority Christian understanding, associated particularly with Irenaeus, that took a different view. It saw primeval innocence as the innocence of childhood and it told the story of human development in terms of a growing up into a not-yet-attained maturity. In these terms, the Fall is more like the stormy times of adolescence. Clearly, an Irenaean account is much more compatible with an evolutionary understanding of terrestrial life than is Augustine's theory of primal catastrophe.

One may picture the developing line of hominid evolution as coming to contain within itself both a dawning of self-consciousness and also a dawning of God-consciousness. At some stage, the lure of the self and the lure of the divine came into competition and there was a turning away from the pole of the divine Other and a turning into the pole of the human ego. Our ancestors became, in Luther's phrase, 'curved in upon themselves'. We are the heirs of that culturally transmitted orientation. One does not need to suppose that this happened in a single decisive act; it would have been a stance that formed and reinforced itself through a succession of choices and actions. Death did not then come into the world for the first time but rather mortality, the sad recognition of human finitude.

Self-consciousness, with its power to envisage the future, made our ancestors able to anticipate that, one day, they would die. At the same time, their increasing alienation from God cut them off from the only true source of hope for a destiny beyond death, thereby making the realization of human transience a bitter one. In such a way it is possible to reconceptualize the Christian doctrine of the Fall.

4

Theism

A nineteenth-century freethinker, who was accused of atheism, once said, 'Tell me who your God is and I will tell you whether I believe in him or not.' He was making the point that the question of the existence of God is not a simply defined issue, comparable to the question of whether unicorns or elephants exist. Many particular concepts of God are held in people's minds. They include a vague notion that there is 'Something behind it all', crudely anthropomorphic images of a celestial wise old man, the idea of a Cosmic Mind, the New Testament belief in the God and Father of our Lord Jesus Christ, and many more. For a sophisticated attempt at a general definition, one could turn to the philosophers of religion. Richard Swinburne summarizes the idea of God as understood in Western religious tradition as relating to a person, omnipotent, omniscient and perfectly free.

The Nature of God

Even if one accepts that definition, there is much unpacking to be done to elucidate its content. God is an infinite being and the language of finite humanity is inevitably inadequate to encompass the divine nature. Theology struggles to find a middle way between, on the one hand, simple acknowledgement of the ineffable mystery of God and, on the other hand, overconfident assertion of an adequate knowledge of the divine nature. The first approach corresponds to what is called 'apophatic theology', the idea that at best one can say what God is not (not finite, not limited in power, and so on) but not what God is. This soon becomes a theology mostly condemned to silence. The second approach is a distortion of what is called 'kataphatic theology', positive statements about the divine nature. Its danger is that it falls into the trap of supposing that God can be contained within the confines of human rational imagining. One possible attempt at an intermediate path is to say that human talk about God is essentially analogical in character, using terms

66

that are 'stretched' in some direction appropriate to the divine infinity, but also in a direction that takes off from an appropriate human starting point.

For example, to speak of God as 'personal' is not to believe in the 'Old Man in the Sky' but to assert that God acts intentionally and specifically in order to achieve divinely chosen purposes. We call God 'Father' and not 'Force' because, though God is at all times everywhere present, God's actions are not the unvarying effect of the kind we associate with, say, the law of gravity, but they are individual and tailored to the precise form appropriate to the particular circumstances.

The other terms in Swinburne's proffered definition also require elucidation. Omnipotence is the assertion that God can do what God wills, that is to say what is in accordance with the divine nature. The rational God cannot be conceived as initiating irrational acts, such as creating a stone too heavy for God to lift, to quote a celebrated puzzle that attracted the attention of medieval theologians, who spent much effort on wrestling with logical conundrums. Omniscience implies that God knows all that can be known. It is a matter of theological dispute whether that includes prior knowledge of the act of a free agent. Does God know today what I shall choose to do tomorrow? The posing of the question in that form raises another matter of contemporary theological debate: God's relationship to time. Is that relationship correctly described as 'eternal', a timeless transcendence of temporality so that the whole of cosmic history is present to God 'at once'? Or is it to be described, rather, as 'everlasting', a divine presence perduring throughout the whole of time, knowing things only as they happen within time? These are issues to which we shall have to return later.

The assertion that God is perfectly free safeguards the divine nature from constraint by any exterior influence whatsoever. God cannot be manipulated by magic. Yet divine freedom should not be understood as implying that God acts with whimsical caprice. Quite the contrary, for the good God only does good acts (the willing of evil is an impossible contradiction in the divine nature); the rational God acts rationally (there could be no divine decree that $2 + 2 = 5$). A theological perplexity arising from these assertions is whether they make goodness and rationality transcendent over God and so deprive God of ultimate status. The classical response, made by thinkers like Aquinas, is the difficult assertion of divine simplicity, the requirement that no distinctions are to be made within God's nature, no separation of God from God's goodness or from God's reason, as if they were independent constituents of the divine nature. So undifferentiated an account has its own problems. For example, divine knowledge must encompass evil, though the divine will utterly rejects it. Thus it seems that a distinction must be drawn between the two, which consequently should not be merged together in divine simplicity. The adequacy of human language is certainly running out here. One solution may be to follow the clue afforded by the theological claim of God's aseity, the divine possession of self-sustaining being-in-itself, so that God owes nothing to any other being for the divine existence. This idea is encapsulated in the theological epigram that in God existence and essence coincide. In a similar way, one might think of God's self-sustaining goodness. In God, the good and the existent coincide.

Scientists are usually wary of philosophical discussion. It seems too 'top-down', too confident of its power rightly to discern general principles. The scientific experience of how surprising the physical world proves to be, of how our ideas have at times to submit to radical revision under the pressure of how things actually are (quantum physics, for instance), makes scientists suspicious of any claim to a prior power in the human mind to judge beforehand what is 'reasonable', or even consistent (wave/particle duality). Instead, scientists prefer 'bottom-up' thinking, starting with the phenomena to be understood and only then seeking to proceed to the principles lying behind the phenomena. The kind of definition given by Swinburne can seem very abstract to the scientific mind. An alternative approach to thinking about God would be to start with the effects in human experience that theistic belief might correspond to or, in other words, to enquire what might be the 'cash value' of belief in God.

Setting aside for the moment individual encounters with the divine presence, which will be considered later when the concept of God's special revelation is discussed, there are a number of general consequences entailed by theistic belief, at least for belief of a kind consonant with Western religious tradition:

- The recognition that there is the mind of a divine Creator behind the pattern and structure of the universe.
- The recognition that there is the will of a divine Creator behind the unfolding history of the universe.
- The recognition that there is One who is worthy of worship and obedience.
- The recognition that there is One who is to be trusted as the ground of an enduring hope.

The bottom-up thinker will want to ask the question of what evidence there might be on which to base such recognitions. We shall discuss some relevant general considerations in this chapter. Insights specific to the Christian tradition will be discussed later, in Chapter 6.

Natural Theology

If God has created the world, one might expect there to be some signs that this is the case. These indications need not be supposed to be plain and unambiguous, as if creatures all bore labels saying 'Made by God', but at least one might anticipate that there would be some hints that could be construed as pointing in a divine direction. Traditionally, the orderliness, continuance and fruitfulness of the world have been appealed to in this way.

Historical Survey

The attempt to learn something of God by such general techniques of enquiry as the exercise of reason and the inspection of the world is the enterprise called 'natural theology'. It is an activity at least as old as the Wisdom writers of the Old Testament. In Christian theological history, there have been two periods in the past when natural theology particularly flourished.

One was the later Middle Ages, with Anselm and Aquinas the leading figures. Their approaches were quite different from each other. Anselm invented the highly ingenious ontological argument. He defined God as that being 'than which no greater can be conceived'. One lists the necessary properties of such a maximal being: omniscience, omnipotence . . . But surely what exists is greater than what does not exist. Therefore existence must be among the divine properties. Hence, God exists!

It is a breathtakingly virtuoso argument, but does it really work? Anselm seems to have done the magic trick of producing a divine rabbit out of a logical top hat. The debate has continued down the centuries and the ontological argument still has its defenders today. Yet many think that Immanuel Kant pointed out the flaw that vitiates the claimed conclusion. Omniscience is a predicate, describing a characteristic that can properly function as part of the specification of an optimal being, but existence is not a predicate in that descriptively signifying sense. Instead it has a different character, as the assertion that there is an actual instantiation of the entity defined by the true predicates. Consequently, it is still an open question whether Anselm's maximal being exists or not (though, no doubt, such a being, if existing, would also possess the property of aseity, of existing independently of any exterior source of being).

The late medievals placed great reliance on logic, about which they thought and argued with considerable acuity. Yet the twentieth century has brought the recognition of the limitations of logical method. We have already noted (p. 60) the work of Kurt Gödel which implied that the consistency of an axiomatized mathematical system is a question that cannot be answered within that system itself. If the consistency of arithmetic cannot be thus demonstrated, it seems unlikely that the question of the existence of God can be answered by the type of purely logical argument that Anselm attempted.

Thomas Aquinas never accepted the validity of the ontological argument. His natural theology was expressed in his famous 'five ways', which look to general features of the world and claim to discern God's necessary presence behind them. Thus, for example, the existence of change, combined with the continuing existence of a world in flux, is held to require an unchanging ground of that world's persistence. In a celebrated phrase, Aquinas concludes that this ground corresponds to 'what all call God'. Only the fifth way, which is an appeal to the design said to be discernible in the aptness of living beings and seen as the expression of the purpose of the divine Designer, makes reference to any very detailed aspect of reality.

The argument from design was pursued with a great wealth of detail in the second great Christian flowering of natural theology, starting towards the end of the eighteenth century. The leading figure was William Paley, whose arguments were perceived as carrying great force, despite criticisms by Hume and Kant of the inadequacy of this line of argument. They had asserted that the world was ambiguous, containing imperfections as well as perfections and, in any case, the design argument (that a watch implies a watchmaker) was too anthropomorphic in character. At best, it could only indicate a powerful but not necessarily infinite Designer, and might there not be more than one of them?

The collapse of this phase of natural theology was not brought about by philosophical criticism, however, but by a scientific discovery. In 1859, Charles Darwin published *The Origin of Species*. It became apparent that there was the possibility of the appearance of design without the need for appeal to the direct action of a Designer. The evolutionary sifting of small differences through natural selection, acting competitively over many generations, was perceived to be capable of producing the observed aptness of living creatures for survival in their environments.

The Revival of Natural Theology

Much twentieth-century theological thinking has been unsympathetic to the idea of a natural theology. Partly that has been because of a wariness induced by the Darwinian episode. Our understanding of the physical world changes and develops and there is a fear that contemporary insight might prove to be as treacherous as Paley's invocation of natural history turned out to be. In Dean Inge's words, 'He who marries the spirit of the age is in danger of soon finding himself a widower.' Partly, also, there has been a reserve about natural theology because of a tendency – particularly marked in the century's greatest theologian, Karl Barth – to believe that the primacy of revelation makes natural theology an exercise that is unnecessary, dangerous and illegitimate.

Nevertheless, a contemporary revival of natural theology is taking place, more at the hands of the physical scientists than at the hands of the theologians. It is, however, a natural theology that is revised in relation to its predecessors in two important respects:

It is more modest in its claims. Its discourse is of insight rather than proof. It does not assert that God's existence can be demonstrated in a logically coercive way (any more than God's non-existence can) but that theism makes more sense of the world, and of human experience, than does atheism. Unbelievers are not fools, but it is held that they explain less than believers can.

Its appeal is not to particular occurrences or particular entities, in contrast to the way in which Paley discussed the optical system of the animal eye or the mechanical aptness of the human hand. The occurrence of such phenomena are part of the history of the physical world that it is science's legitimate role to seek to explain as fully as it can. Instead, the new natural theology looks to the ground of all science's explanation, the laws of nature that it has to take as the assumed and unexplained basis for all its explanation, and it asks whether there is more to be understood about these laws beyond their mere assertion. This new natural theology is in no way a rival to science within science's proper domain. It does not purport to provide answers to what are essentially scientific questions but it serves as a complement to science, going beyond the latter's self-limited realm of enquiry and addressing metaquestions, that arise from scientific experience but which transcend the bounds of scientific understanding alone. There is no recourse here to 'the God of the Gaps' (an appeal to divine explanation to fill in lacunae in current scientific understanding, a disastrous strategy that leads to continual theological retreat in the face of progressing scientific knowledge) but to the God whose steadfast will is held to be expressed in the laws of nature that science discovers but does not explain.

In traditional language, one could say that the new natural theology is concerned with what is called 'the cosmological argument', at root, the discussion of Leibniz's great question, 'Why is there something rather than nothing?' Of course, any explanation has to have its own unexplained basis on which it rests. In relation to total accounts of reality, there are fundamentally just two options for the choice of an explanatory starting point: either the 'brute fact' of the physical world itself, including its natural laws (the solution advocated by Hume), or the 'brute fact' of the will of a divine Agent (the solution of theism). What has given rise to the revival of natural theology is the insight that the laws of nature possess certain characteristics that have resulted in their being seen not to be sufficiently intellectually satisfying and complete in themselves alone. Instead, their form raises questions going beyond science's power to answer, so that they are felt to point beyond science to the need for a deeper and more comprehensive understanding. This feeling is induced by two insistent metaquestions to which we now turn: 'Why is the physical world so intelligible to us?' and 'Why are its laws so finely tuned to the possibility of a fruitful history?' Putting it more briefly, 'Why is science possible?' and 'Why is the universe so special?'

Intelligibility

The universe is astonishingly open to us, rationally transparent to our enquiry. This is what enables scientists to make their discoveries but it is by no means a trivial fact that this is so. One would anticipate that evolutionary selection would produce hominid minds apt for coping with everyday experience, but that these minds should also be able to understand the subatomic world of quantum theory and the cosmic implications of general relativity goes far beyond anything that could conceivably be of relevance to survival fitness. To treat these human powers as just a happy accident, a collateral spin-off from some more direct evolutionary necessity, is to make an unmotivated assertion of highly dubious plausibility and to fail to treat the fact of cosmic intelligibility with the seriousness that it demands.

The mystery deepens when one recognizes that it is mathematics that provides the key to understanding the deep structure of the physical world. It is a technique of proven fruitfulness in fundamental physics to seek those theories whose expression is in terms of beautiful equations. Mathematical beauty is not a property familiar to all but it is one that the mathematical community can discern and reach agreement about. Like all forms of beauty it is easier to recognize than to describe, but it is associated with qualities such as economy, elegance, and something the mathematicians call being 'deep', the discovery of profound consequences inherent in the structure under consideration. Mathematical beauty is valued by physicists, not simply for the aesthetic pleasure it gives, but for its proven fruitfulness as a guide to successful theory choice. Dirac's discoveries in quantum theory and Einstein's discovery of general relativity both resulted from sustained and successful searches for beauti-ful equations.

Mathematics is concerned with abstract exploration by the human mind. Most of its patterns have no ostensible origin in our experience of the world, but nevertheless some of the most aesthetic of them are found to be instantiated in the deep structure of that world. A distinguished theoretical physicist, Eugene Wigner, once called this 'the unreasonable effectiveness of mathematics'. How does it come about that our minds are so perfectly conformed to understanding the universe? It does not seem sufficient to say that this is just our luck.

Some have suggested that humans happen to have a taste for mathe-matics and so they mould their accounts of physics into forms that gratify this preference. Previous discussions of the difficulty of theoretical discovery, and the way in which the universe resists our prior expectation (p. 12), encourage the contrary realist view that these beautiful mathe-matical patterns are read out of, and not read into, the structure of the world.

A metaphysical question such as why the universe is so deeply intelligible to us, with mathematics the key to the unlocking of its secrets, does not lend itself to knock-down answers of a logically coercive kind. The most we can require is an interpretation that is coherent and persuasive. Theism provides just such a response to the metaquestion of intelligibility. If the world is the creation of the rational God, and if we are creatures made in the divine image, then it is entirely understandable that there is an order in the universe that is deeply accessible to our minds. Putting the same point in a different way, one could say that science discerns a world which in its rational beauty and rational transparency is shot through with signs of mind, and the theist can understand this because it is indeed the Mind of God that is partially disclosed in this way. The writers of popular books about cosmology and the like, who are fond of using that kind of language, are, perhaps, speaking better than they know.

The Anthropic Universe

In Chapter 2 we gave an account of the scientific content of the so-called Anthropic Principle and started a preliminary discussion, using John Leslie's 'execution' parable, of what might be its metascientific signifi-cance. To carry the discussion further, it is convenient first to recall two contrasting formulations:

The Weak Anthropic Principle: The laws and circumstances of the universe must be compatible with our presence in it as observers.

This is certainly a weak statement. Its tautological correctness is unchallengeable, but it totally fails to acknowledge the remarkable specificity of a world containing humankind. It amounts to no more than saying 'We're here because we're here', an intellectually lazy response to an unexpectedly precise requirement.

The Strong Anthropic Principle: The universe must be such that it is capable of evolving observers.

This would indeed be a strong statement. It is not clear, however, from whence the necessity asserted is held to originate. Some have suggested that quantum theory requires the eventual existence of observers, but that would seem to confuse conscious observation with macroscopic measurement (see pp. 28–9). The Strong Principle, with its emphatic teleology, could only be a metascientific principle, in which case it would have to be evaluated in relation to the wider metaphysical understanding on which it was based. Before proceeding to discuss further what such a basis might be, there are some preliminary issues to be considered.

First, we have only one universe to observe. How can one conclude anything from a single instance? Yet, with our scientific imaginations we can visit other universes that are 'nearby' to ours in their physical constitution – worlds in which gravity is stronger or electromagnetism weaker than in ours, and so on. In fact, the discussion in Chapter 2 of anthropic precision exactly required mental excursions of this kind. For example, we have every reason to believe that a universe that was identical to ours with the sole exception that gravity was three times stronger would be one in which stars burnt so intensely that their active lives would only last for millions, rather than billions, of years. They could not last long enough to fuel the development of carbon-based life.

Second, it might be that what we now regard as 'finely tuned' coincidences are in fact required to be as they are by a deeper underlying theory. In other words, perhaps things could not be other than we find them to be. In fact, we have already seen something like this happening in the way that inflation is believed to have induced the (anthropically necessary) close balance between cosmic expansion and gravitational attraction. It did not need to be 'written in' at the start, for it is produced by subsequent physical process. Behind the conjecture that there might be more of this going on is the belief, held by some physicists, that there may be only one Grand Unified Theory, because there is only one way in which general relativity and quantum theory can be reconciled with each other. Even if this were so (and it is an uncertain matter, subject to dispute among the experts), one would still have to ask the question of why the universe is gravitational and quantum mechanical. These characteristics are certainly part of anthropic necessity, but they are by no means a logical necessity. A Newtonian world of billiard ball atoms linked together by hooks would be a perfectly consistent, if infertile, possibility. It seems that there will always be something specifically particular about an anthropically fruitful universe. Even if that belief were mistaken, so that for some remarkable reason there was a unique consistent universe, it would still be very striking that that universe proved also to be a fertile one.

Third, much the most difficult criticism of the discussion about the Anthropic Principle is the contention that really it should be called the 'Carbon Principle', since a great deal of the argument centres on the conditions for the evolution of carbon-based life. While that certainly does seem to require a finely tuned physical fabric, might not other universes develop their own idiosyncratic and totally different kinds of fruitful complexity – extended information-processing plasmas, for instance? We understand so little of the physical basis of consciousness that it is impossible to make an assured response to this comment, either positively or negatively. One can only say that those who suppose that different worlds would produce their own different kinds of 'life' are drawing large intellectual blank cheques on unknown intellectual accounts.

It is time to return to Leslie's parable. Anthropic fine tuning is too remarkable to be dismissed as just a happy accident. There are the two interpretative options to consider:

Many worlds. Perhaps there are many different disconnected universes, each with its own natural laws and circumstances. If there are sufficiently many (and there would certainly have to be an enormous number for this line of argument to work), then by chance in one of them conditions will permit the evolution of carbon-based life and that is the one in which we live since we could appear within the history of no other.

Creation. Perhaps there is just one universe which is the way it is in its anthropic fruitfulness because it is the expression of the purposive design of a Creator, who has endowed it with the finely tuned potentiality for life.

Both these propositions are metascientific in character. The many-universes proposal shares this feature with the proposal of a creation, since science only has direct experience of the single universe open to our observation. We have seen that attempts to envisage 'scientific' scenarios for the generation of a portfolio of different worlds (such as the idea of an oscillating universe) invariably have to go beyond what sober science can endorse if they are to provide a sufficient variety of possibilities that might explain the occurrence of an anthropic variant among them. (Technical note: The best that can be achieved by way of using widely accepted scientific ideas to multiply physically realized options is to appeal to the idea of the spontaneous symmetry-breaking which is thought to have occurred in the very early universe as the means by which the hypothesized Grand Unified Theory was reduced to give the presently observed forces of nature. This process need not have been literally universal in effect, but it could have taken different forms in different parts of the universe. This would then have the consequence of there being vast cosmic domains in each of which the actual force constants take different values. We live in that domain in which these force strengths have come out in an anthropically suitable way. It would still be the case, however, that there were significant anthropic constraints on the nature of the aboriginal Grand Unified Theory, necessary to make this scenario possible.)

Metaphysically, in relation to the Anthropic Principle by itself, there does not appear to be anything to choose between the two explanations proffered. Many worlds and creation seem to be of equal plausibility. This ambiguity neatly illustrates the status of natural theology as an insightful, rather than demonstrative, discipline. However, the insight of creation can draw further support if it is perceived as part of a cumulative case for the existence of God, to which the argument from cosmic intelligibility would also contribute. On the other hand, the assumption of many other universes seems to be motivated only by a desire to provide an understanding of anthropic coincidences.

Natural theology of the kind we have been discussing has not only appealed to those of a prior religious persuasion. Someone like Paul Davies, who stands outside any religious tradition, has also argued that more is going on in the universe than is explained by science alone.

A Theology of Nature

While a number of physical scientists have been influenced by the considerations set out in the preceding section, many biological scientists have remained resistant to theistic belief. We have already noted (p. 53) their strongly reductionist tendencies, working against the recognition of a non-material dimension to reality.

Biologists concentrate their attention on an important but localized aspect of cosmic history, the development of life on Earth. They frequently appear to treat as unproblematic the fact that our planet is endowed with the chemical elements necessary for life, and so they pay little attention to the anthropic fine tuning that has made this possible. The rational beauty of the universe, which so impresses the physicists, is not immediately apparent at the biological level. Instead, one has the story of the evolution of life, characterized by random genetic mutations and subjected to the natural selection of those species which survive (at least for a while), profiting from the extinction of their less fit rivals. Only a small fraction of the species that once existed are still alive today. Evolution is a costly business. The biological world is full of both beauty and terror, the handsome leopard preying on the handsome gazelle. The aptness of living creatures to their environment seems not to be the result of skilful design but of painful trial and error. Beneath it all lie simply the operations of chance, random mutations that are mostly deleterious but occasionally, by accident, produce a winning ticket in the lottery of life. Humans may rejoice in nature, but ultimately it is a tale told by an idiot, full of sound and fury, signifying nothing. This is the bleak picture painted for us by atheist biologists such as Jacques Monod and Richard Dawkins.

It is important to recognize two things about this account. The first thing is that it raises questions that theists certainly have to take seriously. The second is that these questions are not scientific in character but metascientific. The equation of 'chance' (which really means historical contingency) with meaninglessness is a metaphysical assertion. It by no means represents the only wider interpretative gloss that can be put upon the purely scientific story.

The discourse of this section differs from that of the preceding section. There we were looking at the laws of nature, the ground rules of the cosmic game, and suggesting that they raised questions going beyond the scientific. It was possible for theism to provide coherent answers to these metaquestions. It was not claimed that these answers were logically inevitable, but that they were insightful and intellectually satisfying. Such a response corresponds to the insights of a modest natural theology, an argument pointing from the world to God. In the dialogue with the biologists, our concern is with the processes and occurrences of the physical world, in particular those of evolutionary biological history. The discussion has moved from the ground rules to the cosmic game itself, as it has actually been played out on planet Earth. The task is to accept the scientific story at its own level but to propose an alternative meta-interpretation of that story, read out from the belief that behind it lie the creative purposes of God. Because of the complexity of the biological story, the argument now being discussed has to point from God to the world. In other words, we are no longer concerned with natural theology but with a theology of nature. The insights of biology are too metaphysically ambiguous to afford the kind of hints of the divine found in fundamental physics, but they are nevertheless capable of being incorporated into a theistic setting.

Monod wrote a famous book entitled *Chance and Necessity*, a slogan that encapsulates a way of thinking about evolutionary process but which, like all slogans, requires a careful elucidation of its constituent terms. We have already seen (pp. 39–40) that necessity corresponds to the lawful regularity of the world, while chance represents historical contingency – the fact that this happened rather than that. There is nothing intrinsically meaningless or inane about chance in this sense of the word, nothing that would carry with it the necessary implication of an idiot universe. 'Chance' simply signifies the particularity of historical process. It is true that genetic mutations are not directly linked to the production of adjustments that would be beneficial in a changing environment, and this observation is what has led some biologists to annexe to chance the tendentious adjective, 'blind'. Yet the process of natural selection is a powerful and flexible means of indirect correlation that the theist can see as being an appropriate way for the Creator to employ as a way of allowing creation to make itself.

The presence of such contingency does, however, suggest that the evolution of life is not the unfolding of a totally predetermined plan. Again, one must be careful to be precise about what this statement means. We must discriminate between specific detail and general tendency. There is no reason to think that it was inherent in the development of terrestrial life that, after four billion years, it should lead precisely to the existence of a being with the exact anatomical and physiological specification of *Homo sapiens*. Many apparently fortuitous events lie between ourselves and the earliest self-replicating molecules. Yet this does not imply that the development of some form of being of a complexity sufficient to sustain self-conscious life was an entirely accidental occurrence. The ideas of Kauffman and others (p. 44) present first steps in the direction of an understanding of the astonishing drive towards increasingly elaborate forms of life, present in evolutionary history, and they encourage the view that this fruitful tendency was inherent in the self-organizing chemical properties of matter, in the same way that these properties themselves were inherent in the quark soup following the big bang. The fundamental potentiality for anthropic fertility was built into the fabric of the universe from the start; its actual form of realization was explored and brought about by the contingency of evolving history.

These insights are consistent with a positive theology of nature. Necessity is seen as the Creator's endowment of creation with the potential for fruitful development. The laws of nature are so designed that they will lead to the coming-to-be of self-conscious and God-conscious beings. However, the precise form of these beings was not laid down by divine decree from all eternity but it results from the operations of chance, the historically contingent development of that fertile endowment, bringing it to a particular fruition. The universe is not God's puppet theatre in which a predetermined script is being inexorably enacted, but it is the arena of improvization in which creation is allowed 'to make itself', to discover and realize its potentiality through the shuffling explorations of possibility. The costliness and blind alleys of evolution are the necessary price to be paid for this open, exploratory creation. (We shall return to this last point when we discuss theodicy in the next chapter.)

Finally, we noted earlier (p. 40) the unresolved ambiguity in the scientific community concerning the answer to the question about the ease with which life can develop, given the necessary physical setting for this to be possible. Some think it is almost inevitable; others that it is so rare a possibility as to make its happening once appear a happy accident. The inescapable ambiguities of metaphysical argument in the biological sphere are neatly illustrated by the reactions to these options that are to be found in the theistic and atheistic communities. If the evolution of life is seen to be almost inevitable, the atheists say that naturalism reigns and there is no need for a Creator, while the theists say that God has so beautifully ordained the order of nature that creation is indeed able to make itself. If life is so rare as to make its occurrence on Earth seem a fortuitous event, the atheists say that it shows that humans have emerged by chance in a world devoid of significance, while theists are encouraged to see the hand of God behind so fruitful but unpredictable an occurrence. Science influences metaphysical understanding but it certainly does not simply determine it. In the end, metaphysical answers are given for metaphysical reasons.

Creation

A theology of nature, as set out in the last section, leads naturally on to a consideration of the doctrine of creation. Much confusion exists in the minds of many because of a false association of creation with the beginning of things. The doctrine of creation is not concerned with temporal origin but with ontological origin. It is proposed as the answer to the question of why anything exists at all, and not to the question of how it all began. God is as much the Creator today as at the instant of the big bang, fifteen billion years ago. Therefore, if Hawking is right in supposing that quantum effects in the very early universe so fuzzed out what was happening that there was not a literal first instant, that is scientifically interesting but theologically negligible. In the same way, big bang cosmology is not a scientific validation of the existence of a Creator, since God's role is not merely initiation but sustaining, holding the universe in being throughout its history, whether that history is finite or infinite in duration.

Creation out of Nothing

The thought of the Creator's sustaining the world in being has traditionally been expressed in Christian theology by the phrase *creatio ex nihilo*, creation out of nothing. It does not mean that God used some peculiar sort of stuff called *nihil* from which to make the universe, but that the universe is at all times held in being, rescued from the abyss of nothingness, by the divine will alone. When quantum cosmologists gaily characterize their notion of the universe as an inflated vacuum fluctuation (pp. 34–6) as being the scientific equivalent of *creatio ex nihilo*, they entirely miss the point. A quantum vacuum is not *nihil*, for it is structured by the laws of quantum mechanics and the equations of the quantum fields involved, all of which the theist will see as existing solely because God decrees that this should be so. There is no area in which the interaction of science and theology is more bedevilled by theological ignorance on the part of scientists than in the discussion of the doctrine of creation.

Continuous Creation

The discovery that the world as we know it did not come into being ready-made but that it has evolved through a long history has enriched Christian discourse about creation. To *creatio ex nihilo* has been added the concept of *creatio continua*, continuing creation unfolding throughout cosmic history. Barbour and Peacocke have discussed this idea in a positive and helpful way. God is present in the evolutionary process – not as its sole determinant, for an evolving world is a creation allowed by its Creator to some degree to 'make itself' through the shuffling explorations of contingency – but as the source and guide of its fruitfulness. The work of the Creator continues, not least through the natural processes that are expressions of God's will. (In the next chapter we shall consider what degree of specific interaction with cosmic process might be held to be exercised by the Creator.) The idea of continuous creation reinforces the understanding that the divine role of Creator is not tied to any particular instant but, on the contrary, it is an enduring relationship.

Creatio continua can be understood as the work of the Creator in the mode of divine immanence, just as *creatio ex nihilo*, the preservation of creation from ontological collapse, is the work of the Creator in the mode of divine transcendence. These theological concepts are consonant with the scientific discernment of a universe of deep order and evolving fruitfulness.

A Wider Humane Reality

Science is only concerned with a small sector of the world of human experience, since it chooses to limit its concern to an impersonal account of reality, the world as an object (an 'it'). It speaks of light of a given wavelength, but not of colour; of vibrations in the air, but not of music; of causal necessity, but not of moral imperative. Yet it is fundamental to human experience that reality is also encountered subjectively (the world as 'thou'). This involves not only interpersonal meeting with other people and the transcendental meeting with the divine, but also the general recognition that we live in a world that is the carrier of value. There is no reason to suppose that these personally appropriated aspects of reality are of lesser significance than the impersonally appropriated aspects that are the concern of science.

Encounters with Value

The fact that value is disregarded by science as its chosen methodological strategy in no way implies that this neglect should be elevated into a metaphysical principle. On the contrary, any adequate metaphysics will have to take account of the value-laden character of reality.

Ethical intuitions. Subjectively discerned qualities, such as ethical obligations, are always more open to the effects of cultural distortion than are the 'objective' quantities that science purports to discuss (but see p. 12). Anthropologists report the immense variety of human perceptions and assessments of moral worth, drawing our attention to tribes like the Ik of Uganda whose way of life appears to be based on an unyielding selfishness. Nevertheless, many find it impossible to believe that statements such as 'torturing children is wrong', 'compassion is better than hatred', are simply social conventions of the societies within which they are uttered. We do seem to have access to real moral knowledge. It affords us a window into a world of humane reality.

Aesthetic experience. Another window into that world is provided by human experiences of beauty. How does it come about that arrangements of specks of paint, or sequences of sound waves in the air, convey to us an encounter with a dimension of reality too profound to be dismissed as merely epiphenomenal froth on the surface of an intrinsically valueless world? Again, there are culturally formed elements that influence human experiences of beauty, but which do not seem to reduce them merely to conventionalized interpretations of intrinsically value-free events. Something of lasting significance is glimpsed in the beauty of the natural world and the beauty of the fruits of human creativity.

Theistic belief offers an explanation of the widespread presence of value in the world. Human ethical intuitions are understood as originating in intimations of God's good and perfect will; encounters with beauty are understood as arising from a sharing in the Creator's joy in creation. Here is the experiential basis for the recognition that there is One worthy of worship and obedience, who is the ground of the aesthetic and moral worth of the world. This theistic appeal to value is a version of the 'fourth way' of Thomas Aquinas: 'Therefore there must also be something which to all things is the cause of their being, goodness and perfection; and this all call God.'

Intimations of Hope

Despite the pain and suffering of the world, there is a deep human intuition that, in the end, all will be well, that ultimately history makes sense. Peter Berger, in his analysis of 'signals of transcendence' present in everyday life, draws our attention to the phenomenon of a parent comforting a frightened child who has woken up from a nightmare. The mother or father conveys to that child the reassurance necessary for its humane development by saying, 'It's all right.' Berger asks the question whether this is a loving lie or a deep insight into the nature of reality. He suggests that it is the latter, a sign of the hope that lies at the heart of humanity, notwithstanding the bitterness present in human experience.

Despite the inescapable fact of mortality, there is a deep human intuition that the last word does not lie with death. The German atheist philosopher, Max Horkheimer, spoke of the need that the murderer should not triumph over his innocent victim.

These intimations of hope are the experiential basis for the recognition that there is One who is to be trusted as the ground of an enduring hope. The claim that we live in a cosmos, a universe that makes total sense, requires belief in a God who is not subject to the futility and decay that eventually leads to the frustration of all this-worldly becoming. The Christian articulation of this eschatological hope will be discussed in Chapter 6.

Conclusion

The coming-to-be of persons, self-conscious individuals with the range of humane experience we have sketched in this section, is surely the most significant development in cosmic history that is known to us. No metaphysics would begin to be adequate that does not treat this fact with the seriousness it demands. It has been suggested that theism provides insightful understanding of the phenomenon and that there is an humanities-based form of natural theology that can function alongside the more familiar science-based natural theology discussed under 'Natural Theology'. This brief survey of 'A Wider Humane Reality' is as far as we can carry the matter in a book devoted principally to the interaction of science and theology.

5

Divine Action

Even at its most persuasive, natural theology can only lead to a limited concept of God as the Great Architect of the Universe, the One whose mind and will are behind cosmic order and fruitfulness, but no more than that. Since natural theology is based on limited considerations, it is scarcely surprising that its conclusions should yield only limited insight. It is as consistent with the God of deism (a Creator who brought the world into being and then simply left it to its own devices) as it is with the Judaeo-Christian-Islamic God who is active within creation.

The concept of continuous creation, if it is really to mean something, seems to require a strong account of God's relation to the world. The idea should amount to more than merely a pious gloss imposed on a fundamentally natural evolutionary story. There must be divine activity actually present in the development of life if it is properly to be called continuous creation. One might expect that activity to amount to more than simply a sustaining of the underlying natural laws that make evolution possible. In other words, one should look for God's presence in the historical contingency (chance) as well as in the regularity (necessity) of what is happening.

Though the language used is no doubt stretched, the concept of a personal God surely implies that God does particular things in particular circumstances. These considerations raise the issue of the extent to which we can, with integrity, suppose God to act in the universe as science describes it. Is the net of physical causality drawn too tight to allow for the specific actions of a divine Agent? The fact that human agency is also exercised within the same physical world encourages the thought that this need not be so.

In speaking of divine action, one can discriminate between three levels of specificity:

General providence. This is the divine sustaining of the order of the world, in which the laws of nature are understood as expressions of God's faithfulness. The deist, as much as the theist, will accept this concept.

Special providence. This is concerned with particular divine actions within cosmic history. They are understood to take place within the grain of physical process and so they are not immediately distinguishable from other happenings. God may act through famine or through times of plenty, and this may be discernible by faith, but it will not be demonstrable to the sceptic.

Miracle. This is concerned with radically unnatural events, such as turning water into wine or restoring the dead to life. If such things happen, their very nature suggests that they are the effects of divine action of an unusual kind.

These categories are not entirely sharply defined. There are some events (such as those that might be interpretable as highly significant coincidences) which might seem to fall into a grey borderline area. Nevertheless, the classification provides a useful taxonomy for thinking about possible divine acts.

There has been much discussion of God's action in recent writing about science and theology. We proceed to survey some of the suggestions that have been made.

Single Action

Theologians like Gordon Kaufman and Maurice Wiles have proposed that the best way to think of God's relationship to creation is in terms of the single timeless act of sustaining cosmic history. On this view, there is only general providence. God is in the overall necessity, but the detailed happenstance of actual historical process is just how it all chances to work out.

Two motivations appear to lie behind this minimalist account. One is the feeling that the integrity of modern science would be breached in an arbitrary way by any other suggestion. With the death of a merely mechanical picture of physical process, this is by no means clearly the case, a point to which we shall return below. The second motive is a desire to find some solution to the problem of theodicy by absolving the divine will of responsibility for the actual evil and suffering present in creation. The God of the single great act does nothing in particular, and so cannot be held responsible for anything in particular. Such a solution would seem, however, to be a pyrrhic victory for theology, for why has God chosen so detached and indifferent a stance? Is that not in itself culpable? Yet one

85

must acknowledge that the stronger one's account of divine action, the more pressing becomes the problem of theodicy. This is another point to which we shall return. In the meantime, one can note that the atemporal deism of Kaufman and Wiles is hard to reconcile with religious experiences of prayer and of the prophetic discernment of a divine special providence at work in history.

Primary Causality

A position similar to single action in its consequences for human accounts of physical process, but totally opposed to it in its metaphysical interpretation, is the claim that God acts by a primary causality exercised in and under the unriven network of creaturely secondary causality. No 'causal joint' can be exhibited by means of which the Creator acts upon creation, but the divine agency is ineffably present as the source of all that happens. This is a theological tradition at least as old as Thomas Aquinas and it has had its twentieth-century defenders, notably Austin Farrer.

The attraction of this stance is that it leaves science free to give what account it will of secondary causes, treating the detail of that account as being of no significance to the understanding of divine action. Theology is rendered invulnerable to any scientific description of physical process, whatsoever it may be. There are, however, two problems about primary causality. The first concerns its intelligibility. No explanation is offered of how it all works. Indeed, the search for an explanatory causal joint is declared to be futile, verging almost on the blasphemous. This leaves the idea looking like mere fideistic assertion, compatible with any known facts about the way things happen and so lacking any interpretative force in relation to the way things happen. It may be the case that the problem of divine action is humanly insoluble (cf. p. 56), but that should be a position of last resort, retreated to only after all other explanatory strategies have been tried and found wanting.

The second difficulty is that primary causality makes God directly responsible for all that happens, thereby intensifying the problems of theodicy. The proposal arose within a tradition that wished to speak in strong terms of the Creator's almighty control of creation, but that may prove to be a price too high for theology to pay in the century of the Holocaust.

Process Thought

Process thought has its own distinctive way of accommodating divine action. God is seen as being a participant in each actual occasion, bringing to the event the record of past experience, the portfolio of possible outcomes, and presenting the 'lure', enticing the result in a divinely desired direction. Nevertheless, the actual outcome derives from the concrescent phase of the event itself. God's power is simply the power of persuasion. Whitehead reacted strongly against what he saw as classical theology's account of the Cosmic Tyrant. In its place he put the concept of God as 'the fellow sufferer who understands', a pleading participant, but not a determinator, in the process of reality.

The scientific difficulty of relating process thought's event-dominated account of reality to what we know about the physical world has already been noted (p. 56). To this must now be added the theological difficulty of whether process ideas can give a sufficiently strong account of divine action to satisfy the theistic requirement of taking seriously the insight of God's special providence at work in history. Is the Pleader on the margin of occurrence a concept adequate to the religious experience of prayer or to the hopeful intuition that in the end the good will triumph over the bad? Barbour has been frank enough to acknowledge that process theology cannot necessarily assert an eventual divine triumph over evil. Its hope is framed in terms of a divine remembrance of what is past, rather than the transformation of the imperfect present into future eschatological fulfilment.

Analogies with Human Agency

Since our own actions are the form of agency best known to us, it has been natural to seek to exploit a possible analogy between human and divine agency. This strategy faces two difficulties. One is the general problem of the extent to which finite human experience can be used as a guide to speaking about the infinite reality of God. The other is that, though we have direct experience of our own power to act, the way this happens is still mysterious to us. We do not understand in any agreed way the nature of the causal joint by which human agency is exercised (Chapter 3). The approach of this section is therefore something of an appeal from the unknown to the Unknown.

Embodiment

Much the bluntest version of this strategy is to regard God as being embodied in the universe as the Mind or Soul of the world. Divine action would then be the analogue of the way in which we act in our bodies (whatever that may be). The account does not have to be framed in pantheistic terms (equating God and the universe), for it is also compatible with a form of panentheism, the assertion that God contains the universe but transcends it, so that the world is in God but God exceeds the world.

The plausibility of this view is open to question. The universe may not look like a mechanism but it does not look like an organism either, lacking the degree of intricate interrelationship that characterizes the parts of a living being. Humans are constituted by their bodies, whose decay brings about their death. It is hard to believe that God is in any significant way constituted by the cosmos. Scientifically, the universe appears to have had a finite past; it has undergone several radical transformations in the course of its evolution; its history will end in collapse or decay. None of these characteristics seem readily compatible with divine embodiment.

Top-Down Causality

Some writers, such as Arthur Peacocke, have thought in a different way about panentheism, declining the use of the language of embodiment. An alternative idea to pursue is that of top-down causality, the influence of the whole upon the parts, as opposed to bottom-up causality, the effect of individual parts upon the whole. When a person raises their arm, though the action has associated with it neural currents and muscular contractions, it also seems to be an act of the whole individual, in just such a top-down fashion. The spontaneous generation of large-scale order out of chaos (pp. 43–4), involving the coordinated motions of trillions of molecules, may also be thought to have something of this top-down character to it. Could it not be that God acts in an analogous way on the universe as a whole? If this account of divine action is to succeed in making terrestrial special providence intelligible, one must suppose that this cosmic influence trickles down to produce localized consequences on planet Earth. Peacocke sometimes speaks of God as 'the boundary condition of the universe', but it is not entirely clear what this could mean.

Top-down causality, despite our direct experience of it, is not an unproblematic concept. If it exists as a genuine causal principle, this must imply that the nexus of bottom-up causality is not drawn so tight as to exclude room for the influence of the whole upon the parts (cf. contextualism, p. 51). Once more, we return to the question of the causal joint, the problem of how physical process might accommodate the holistic effects of human and divine agency.

An Open Universe

Possible sources of openness in physical process are quantum theory and chaos theory. In each case, the undoubted unpredictabilities would have to be interpreted in an ontological sense, as signals of an underlying ontological openness.

The move to associate divine action with quantum indeterminacy is at least as old as the writings of William Pollard in the 1950s, and it has some contemporary supporters today. At first sight, subatomic processes might appear the antithesis of global top-down interaction. Certainly, some enhancement mechanism would be needed to promote microscopic effects into macroscopic consequences, a point on which no detailed proposals seem to have been made. There is a further difficulty. The unpredictabilities of quantum processes relate solely to the outcomes of measurements (of course, not necessarily consciously observed). The proposal is that God should determine some, at least, of these results. In between measurements, quantum theory is perfectly deterministic, the wave function evolving smoothly in time according to the Schrödinger equation. Thus, if divine action is exerted through quantum effects, it will not be continuous but episodic. Such occasional divine activity seems open to theological objection.

The proposal that an ontologically interpreted chaos theory might be a way of thinking about human and divine agency has been proposed by Polkinghorne. Active information might prove to be the scientific equivalent of the immanent working of the Spirit on the 'inside' of creation. The spiritual character of divine influence would correspond to pure input of information (a proposal first made in general terms by John Bowker), with the absence of energetic input delivering the concept from the theologically unacceptable character of making God just an invisible cause among physical causes. Some confusion has arisen about this last assertion. There are theorems relating the transmission of information (in the sense of communication theory, as used by telephone engineers) to an irreducible expenditure of energy, necessary to make the signal rise above the background noise. This consideration, however, is not relevant to pattern-forming active information, so that divine action through pure information input seems a consistent possibility.

Like all suggestions concerning divine action, this proposal lacks a fully articulated account. With present understanding, all that seems possible in this area is the framing of hopeful conjectures. Another form of conjecture might appear to be to combine the two previous proposals by using chaotic sensitivity to fine details as a means of promoting the consequences of quantum openness into the macroscopic realm. After all, chaotic systems soon become dependent on effects at the level of Heisenberg uncertainty. There are, however, two problems with this strategy. One is that the relationship between the microscopic quantum world and the macroscopic everyday world is not well understood (technically, this is 'the measurement problem' in quantum theory). The other is that the quantum equivalent of chaotic systems has not been successfully identified. These technical difficulties make such a hybrid approach problematic.

Any account of God's agency that locates the causal joint within the cloudiness of unpredictable physical process has the consequence that acts of special providence cannot be isolated and itemized. It is not possible to disentangle the causal web, asserting that God did this, a human person did that, and nature did the other thing. Faith may be able to discern but inspection cannot demonstrate divine action of this kind. There are also realms of physical process that are free from unpredictable ambiguity, such as the rotation of the Earth and the succession of the seasons. Phenomena of this kind will be undisturbed in their regularity, serving as signs of the faithfulness of the Creator.

Divine Temporality

Closely connected to the consideration of issues of divine action is the question of how God relates to a temporal creation. We have already encountered the metascientific dispute about the alternatives of a block universe or a temporal world of true becoming (pp. 47–8).

Augustine and Boethius gave expression to the belief of classical theism that God perceives the whole of cosmic history 'at once', in a timeless act of knowing by the One who is outside time altogether. Since God surely knows things according to their true natures, this would seem to imply theological endorsement of the concept of the block universe. There is no logically necessary connection between such a block universe and the question of the open or deterministic character of its physical process. In fact, Aquinas insisted that God's simultaneous knowledge of all history abolished divine *fore*knowledge and so made total divine omniscience compatible with the free acts of created agents, since such acts can be known contemporaneously but not in advance. Nevertheless, there is a certain degree of alogical association between an atemporal view and determinism, and between temporality and openness.

The open universe of the last section would be a world of true becoming. The future is not up ahead, awaiting our arrival so to speak, but we make it as we go along. If this is correct, it would seem that God would know that world in its temporal becomingness. A great variety of theological thinkers in the twentieth century, ranging from Karl Barth to the scientist-theologians, have wished to assert, for a great variety of reasons, that there is temporal experience located in the Godhead, in addition to divine eternity. A dipolar theism of time/eternity has been a major item on the contemporary theological agenda. It is a central belief of process theology but it draws support also from a much wider community of thinkers.

A much more disputed corollary to this view is the belief that it implies God's acceptance of a self-restriction on the scope of divine omniscience. God must know all that can be known, but if the future does not yet exist, even God cannot yet know it. This leads to the concept of current omniscience: God knows now all that can be known now, but not yet all that will eventually be knowable.

The way God is believed to relate to time will also tend to influence, but again not with logical necessity, how divine action is conceived to occur. The total knowledge of all history enjoyed by the atemporal God of Augustine and Boethius is so different from human enmeshment in time that it discourages the search for analogies between human and divine agency. It is scarcely surprising that classical theism endorsed the ineffable idea of primary causality. On the other hand, if both God and humanity participate in the evolving temporality of a universe of becoming, then the search for analogies receives some degree of encouragment.

Finally, one must consider the question raised by relativity theory's recognition of the observer-related character of temporal experience. What time is God's time or, more technically, what is God's frame of reference? The issue is not quite so critical as it might at first appear. God is not a localized observer, but everywhere present. Whatever the divine time axis might be, the frame of God's omnipresence will sweep out the whole of cosmic history, so that God experiences every event as and when it happens. Divine respect for the integrity of creation will surely imply that God will not exploit the possibilities for superluminal signalling, inherent in omnipresence, to subvert the ordained causal order of the universe. Finally there is, in fact, in our kind of universe a natural frame of reference that might well be associated with its Creator, namely that at

91

rest with respect to the background radiation, the same frame that cosmologists use to define the age of the universe.

Miracle

Special providence is concerned with divine actions that can be construed as lying within the grain of natural process. Religious traditions also contain claims for divine acts of so remarkable a character that they seem to run totally contrary to any natural expectation. The question of miracle in this radical sense is specially relevant to Christian theology because of the central role of Christ's resurrection in its thinking. No one could suppose that a dead man came alive, never to die again, through some clever divine exploitation of quantum theory or chaotic dynamics. Our concern here will be with the general question of whether it is possible, with integrity, to believe that any such miraculous events could actually have occurred, postponing till the next chapter the discussion of any specific claim, such as that of the resurrection of Christ.

By their nature, miracles are unique events and not recurrent phenomena. They lie, therefore, outside the normal scope of scientific enquiry, which is concerned with what usually occurs and what can be made the subject of repeatable investigation. Strictly speaking, science cannot exclude the one-off, though the more it discerns a regular world, the more problematic become the claims for such unique occurrences. The main problem about miracle is, however, theological.

It is theologically incredible that God acts as a kind of celestial conjurer, doing occasional tricks to astonish people but most of the time not bothering. Such a capricious notion of divine action is totally unacceptable. The main problem of miracle, from the theological point of view, is how such wholly exceptional events can be reconciled with divine consistency.

God's self-consistency is the self-consistency of a 'person'. It does not imply a dreary uniformity. In unprecedented circumstances, God may well act in unprecedented ways. Theology can borrow from science the concept of a regime, a domain of experience characterized in some intrinsically significant way. It is a familiar fact that a change of regime can produce dramatic changes of behaviour, as in the transition in metals from the conducting state to the superconducting state, resulting in the total vanishing of electrical resistance. Physicists call these radical transformations 'phase changes'. Even the boiling of water, the transition at 100 degrees Celsius from the liquid regime to the gaseous regime, would astonish us if we had not seen it happen several times every day. The laws of nature do not change at these transition points but their consequences do so dramatically. There is superficial discontinuity (even to the point of apparent irrationality in the vanishing of electrical resistance) but underlying continuity.

The theological attempt to understand miracle must seek to pursue a similar strategy. Miracles are not to be interpreted as divine acts against the laws of nature (for those laws are themselves expressions of God's will) but as more profound revelations of the character of the divine relationship to creation. To be credible, miracles must convey a deeper understanding than could have been obtained without them. Hence the language of 'signs' used in the fourth Gospel. The satisfaction of this theological criterion has to be evaluated event by event, for there is no general theory of exceptional happenings. The process will be illustrated by the discussion of the resurrection in Chapter 6.

Theodicy

If God does indeed act in the world, it is necessary to go on to ask the question why such action is not more extensive and effective. There is so much evil and suffering that seems to cry out for divine amelioration. There are two types of evil to be considered:

Physical evil, the disease and disaster that make life painful and hazardous. Though the effects of physical evil can be enhanced by human heedlessness (as when schools and hospitals are built on earthquake fault lines because the land is cheap), most of the responsibility for its existence seems to lie with the Creator.

Moral evil, the wilfully chosen bad actions of humankind, for which the prime responsibility must lie with the perpetrators. One may ask why God did not stop the Holocaust, but one must also recognize that it was directly brought about by the decisions of evil people and by the compliance of a political system unduly submissive to the will of the state.

There are two basic strategies to which theodicy can have recourse. The first is to deny or diminish the reality of evil. The classical statement of this position is Augustine's account of evil as 'the privation of the good'. He held that, just as darkness is not a positive quality but the absence of light, so evil is not a positive quality but the absence of goodness. In this century of suffering, this seems altogether too blithe a theory, failing to acknowledge the terrible intensity with which evil has been experienced.

93

The second strategy is to claim that bad things happen as the necessary cost of other very good things. The celebrated 'free-will defence' in relation to moral evil is an example of this kind of argument. It claims that it is better for creation to contain freely choosing persons, however disastrous some of their choices may prove to be, than to be populated with perfectly programmed automata. What we call 'character' cannot be ready-made, but it must be formed through a history of moral decisions. In such a free world, there must be the possibility of evil choices being made as well as good choices. The existence of moral evil is then seen to be the necessary cost of the existence of the greater good of human freedom and moral responsibility.

Polkinghorne has suggested that there is an analogous 'free-process defence' in relation to physical evil. A world allowed to make itself through the evolutionary exploration of its potentiality is a better world than one produced ready-made by divine fiat. In such an evolving world there must be malfunctions and blind alleys. The same biochemical processes that enable some cells to mutate and produce new forms of life will allow other cells to mutate and become malignant. Entities will behave in accordance with their natures, as when a tectonic plate slips and causes a devastating earthquake.

The arguments of theodicy cannot be claimed to produce a total explanation of the profound mystery of suffering. A number of comments need to be made:

A great deal of the perplexity arises from *the scale of the problem*. A totally risk-free world might be so bland as to fail to stimulate human spiritual growth and development. Some challenge from danger and difficulty can be seen as constituent of what it is to be human (think of dangerous pastimes such as mountain climbing). Yet the weight of suffering seems often to exceed what can be borne, crushing those on whom it falls. Some rise above the impact of evil in a way that is inspiring, but others are diminished by it to the point almost of the extinction of their humanity.

One might challenge the *legitimacy of the use of the word 'free' in the free-process defence*, seeing it as an abuse of language. Tectonic plates are not moral beings, requiring freedom from divine interference if they are to fulfil their nature. Nevertheless, humanity is so intimately connected with the physical world that gave it birth, that it might be thought that only a universe to which the free-process defence applied could give rise to beings subject to the free-will defence.

There are further specific Christian responses to the problem of evil and suffering, including God's own participation through Christ in the painful process of creation, together with the hope of healing and fulfilment in a destiny beyond death, to which consideration will be given in the following chapter.

Theological discussion of theodicy is strongly dialectic in character, taking place at the meeting place of opposites:

Chance and necessity. Historical contingency is God's gift to creation of the power to make itself; lawful necessity is God's gift of dependability. Fruitfulness and frustration are both consequence of the resulting inter-play. We have already noted that an evolving world must also contain the possibility of cancer. Its presence is not a sign of divine incompetence or callousness.

Grace and free will. God acts but does not overrule. The Spirit guides, but with a gentle respect for the integrity of creation. The act of murder and the incidence of cancer may both be thought to be contrary to the divine will, but they are allowed to happen by divine permission in a world that is not the creation of the Cosmic Tyrant.

The classic statement of the dilemma of theodicy is to ask how a God both all-loving and almighty could produce a creation experienced as such a vale of tears. Christian theology has retained its belief in divine benevolence but it has been prepared to nuance its understanding of what it means to call God 'almighty'. God can indeed do anything that is in accordance with the divine will, but it would not be consonant with that will to create a world that is merely God's puppet theatre. Instead there is a divine letting-be, a making room for the created-other, together with the acceptance of the consequences that will flow from free process and from the exercise of human free will.

6

Christian Theology

Almost all believers in God are not theists in some general philosophical sense but they are adherents of one of the world's great faith traditions. Three of these traditions – Judaism, Christianity and Islam – are closely linked together, not only by historical and geographical connections of origin, but also by a common attitude to certain major theological issues. All three, in their classical expressions:

- take the reality of the physical world with great seriousness (not least because their followers made substantial contributions to the initial development of modern science);
- acknowledge the significance and great value in God's sight of the individual human person;
- believe that there is a divine will and purpose behind the unfolding history of the universe;
- trust in a powerful and compassionate God who acts within the history of creation in specific providential ways.

All three traditions, therefore, take broadly comparable positions in relation to the topics of the preceding chapters and they would be likely to share in the general understanding of the relationship between science and theology so far set out. Yet each tradition would not feel that its understanding of God was at all adequately articulated by such a common-denominator account alone. There are important further things to be said, and in the saying of them the traditions begin to diverge from each other in significant ways.

For Judaism, the Jews are God's chosen people, elected in Abraham and made into a nation through their divine deliverance from slavery in Egypt. God's covenant with Israel was ratified by the giving of the Law (*Torah*) to Moses at Mount Sinai, and the implications of that gift have been drawn out through centuries of rabbinic reflection and argument concerning what follows for human understanding and, above all, for human conduct (*halakah*).

For Christianity, God has manifested the divine nature finally and definitely in Jesus Christ. He is the unique meeting point between humanity and divinity. The Chuch's tradition represents the appropriation, through worship and prayerful reflection, of what was given in the foundational events recorded in the New Testament.

For Islam, God's actual words, spoken in heaven and conveyed to Mohammed by an angel, are recorded in the pages of the Qur'an. No truly adequate translation of this sacred text is possible; it must be read in the original classical Arabic, the very words that God chose to use.

Not only do the traditions diverge and contradict each other in these and other ways, but they also have differing methods of theological discourse: rabbinical argument, Christian appeal to history and reason, Islamic exposition of a divinely originated text. If one adds to the cousinly discords of the Abrahamic faiths, the further disparities represented by the indigenous religions of India, China and Japan (not all of which are theistic), a bewildering picture of religious diversity results. This is in striking contrast to the worldwide acceptance that has been accorded to modern science. While historically different cultures have displayed varying degrees of interest in the physical world, and formed varying accounts of its nature and process, the scientific child of seventeenth-century Europe has been adopted and given a home almost universally. The 'archaic' religions of indigenous peoples may represent pockets of resistance – and some Westerners believe that alternative insights of great value are preserved in this way – but, generally speaking, the single voice of science contrasts markedly with the dissonant voices of the religions. There is increasing recognition that the interaction of science and theology cannot continue satisfactorily without giving serious consideration to the issue of religious diversity.

Our discussion of the matter will proceed in two stages. The first, with which this chapter is concerned, will be the exploration of a particular religious tradition, namely Christianity. Religion as a cultural or anthropological phenomenon can be studied from the outside in a comparative and descriptive way, recording what different people say and do. But religion as a theological phenomenon (that is to say, religion in its essence) cannot be assessed with such detachment. There is no theological Archimedean point from which the traditions may be surveyed with accuracy and with academic impartiality. They can only really be known from the inside, by their adherents. This book has a Christian author and it would be disingenuous to pretend otherwise. The purpose of this chapter, therefore, will be to illustrate how someone with the experience and habits of thought of a scientist approaches central questions of specifically Christian belief. There is no unique way of doing this and comparisons will sometimes be drawn with other writers with a similar general background, like Barbour and Peacocke. This will lead to a reconsideration at the end of the chapter of issues raised briefly in Chapter 1 (pp. 20–2).

The second stage then moves out from this Christian platform to consider the interrelationships of the world faith traditions. In accordance with what has already been said about the impossibility of complete detachment, a Christian perspective is still present, but it is by no means claimed that this is the only possible viewing point or that all that is discernible of the divine mystery can be seen from it. This ecumenical enquiry will be the subject of Chapter 7.

Revelation

Chapter 1 suggested that revelation, understood as a specific source of knowledge of God, is best considered in analogy with the role of experiments in science. Though the laws of nature are always operating, experiments are events in which they are specially readily discernible. Similarly, revelation consists in those persons and happenings in which the divine presence, though always there, is specially readily discernible. There is an important distinction, however. Experiments are brought about by human contrivance; encounter with God comes as gracious gift. It is the serious error called 'magic' to try to enforce manifestations of the divine. Another significant, and related, difference lies in the unique character of personal encounter, contrasted with the repeatable character of impersonal experiments. Yet, just as the individual creative insight of the artist can, through painting, music or literature, resonate with and reinforce the lesser insights of ordinary people, so the record of a unique revelatory event can induce an illuminating response in generations of religious seekers. The continuing deposit of the record of transpersonal encounters with God is to be found in scripture and tradition.

Scripture

All religious traditions possess writings that are accorded the status of scripture and which thereby play a normative role in that tradition's theological thinking. One could classify Christian attitudes to the Bible along the lines of Lindbeck's taxonomy of ways of doing theology (pp. 18–19):

A cognitive approach would encourage treating the Bible as the source of authoritative propositions. At its most fundamentalist, this could lead to the citation of 'proof texts' in ways that may pay scant attention to context, and it might lead to desperate attempts to prove the total inner consistency of a collection of writings compiled over a period of more than a thousand years and originating in many different historical and cultural settings.

An expressive approach would encourage treating the Bible as a source of spiritual inspiration. At its most sentimental, this could lead to the selection of heart-warming passages, selected according to taste, and result in the discarding of difficult and uncongenial material.

A cultural approach would encourage treating the Bible as the story book of the Christian community. At its most literary, this could lead to a disregard of historical questions and result in an undue concentration on the category of myth.

The Bible certainly contains truth about God; it certainly has moved many people to lives of spiritual depth and to deeds of great generosity; it certainly is an indispensable symbolic resource of Christian discourse. Yet it also contains unedifying material concerned with acts of genocide portrayed as divine commands, vengeful curses upon enemies, sadistic symbols of everlasting torture.

Any adequate and honest approach to the Bible will have to take account of all these features. The concept of a '*critical realist*' approach to the Bible may provide the way of doing so. The normative and authoritative status of the Old and New Testaments derives from their being the records of the foundational events of God's self-disclosure in the history of Israel and in the life, death and resurrection of Jesus Christ. Israel was an insignificant small nation, repeatedly caught in the crossfire of the great states (Egypt, Assyria, Babylon) that competed across the Fertile Crescent. In geopolitical terms it has left little deposit in Middle Eastern history. Its significance lies precisely in its encounter with God. Without that, the ancient Israelites would be as little known and remembered as the Hivites and Perrizites that they displaced from the land of Canaan.

Jesus was a wandering unofficial teacher, prophet and wonder-worker in a frontier province of the Roman Empire. He left virtually no mark on contemporary secular history. His significance lies precisely in the claims made for God's unique presence in him (to be considered shortly). Without that claim, he would be like other charismatic figures from the ancient world, such as Appolonius of Tyana or Honi the circle-drawer, at best known only to a few scholars.

A prime role for the Bible is its being read as historical evidence to be assessed in relation to the large claims made by Christianity about the religious significance of Israel and Jesus of Nazareth. Just as theory and experiment inextricably intertwine in science, so the biblical accounts are interpreted accounts, seeking to convey the inner meaning of Israelite history and to support the central Christian claim that the myth of God's sharing with humanity in the embracing and redeeming of suffering is an historically enacted myth, actually lived out in Jesus. Just as background effects cloud our experimental vision of the reaction that is being studied, so time-based, limited cultural attitudes (to women, war and much else besides) cloud the Bible's vision of the eternal truth to which it nevertheless bears essential witness. Just as Newton must give way to Einstein and Bohr, so there is a paradigm shift between the early tribes of Israel with their local deity YHWH, and the later understanding of one universal Lord of all the Earth who wills the salvation of the whole of humanity. Just as quantum theory is forced by its actual experience to wrestle with the strange duality of wave and particle, so Christian theology is forced by its actual experience of the risen Christ to wrestle with the strange duality of humanity and divinity. It is this critical realist understanding of the role of Scripture that will control the discussion that follows.

Tradition

The ancient writings of the Bible share with the classics of literature the power to speak across the centuries. They do so because they penetrate beneath the superficialities of contingent culture to the deep structure of human nature. In a famous phrase drawn from hermeneutics (the study of the interpretation of texts), they fuse 'the two horizons' of the past and the present into one experience of shared insight. Involved is a resonance between what was experienced then and what is being experienced now.

Scripture is not the dead record of the past but it must function in the living present. The foundational revelatory events cannot be repeated but they have to be reappropriated in each generation. This continuing exploration of the ongoing encounter with God is deposited in the living tradition of the Church, within which Scripture is read and understood and within which Scripture itself was originally identified. The books that comprise the Hebrew Bible (Old Testament) and the New Testament emerged with the endorsement of the Jewish and Christian communities respectively, after a winnowing process that lasted several centuries. The convivial act of communal judgement, which Polanyi identified as taking place in the invisible college of scientists, is paralleled in the sifting and authenticating of religious experience in the community of the faithful.

Religious experience — the meeting with the sacred — takes a number of forms:

Mystical. Widely attested in all religious traditions, mysticism, properly understood, is not a vague and fanciful religiosity but an intense experience of unity, described as being either with the One (an encounter with the ineffable mystery of God) or with the All (an identification with the totality of the real). There is a striking similarity in the accounts that the mystics give, from whatever religious tradition or whatever century they come. William James expressed this universality by saying that the mystics have 'neither birthday nor native land'. A Christian theologian will understand mystical experience as encounter with God in the mode of immanence.

Numinous. The complementary encounter with divine transcendence lies in the numinous meeting with the Holy One, the tremendous, overwhelming, awe-inspiring experience of finitude in the presence of the Infinite. A classical biblical account of the phenomenon is Isaiah's vision in the Temple, when he saw the Lord, high and lifted up, an experience that induced in him an intense feeling of his own sinful unworthiness (Isa. 6.1–8). Once again, numinous experience is to be found in all religious traditions but it is, perhaps, particularly attested in the Abrahamic faiths, with their emphasis on the holiness of a personal God, the King of the universe.

Prayer and worship. Many religious people will not have had experiences of the intensity of the mystical or the numinous, yet they will wish to give their testimony to a lower-key experience of awareness of the divine presence. Personal prayer (including a disciplined still waiting on God) and public worship (including for the Christian the Eucharist, the sacrament of Christ's body and blood) will frequently be the occasions of this kind of meeting with God.

Desolation. Experiences of a feeling of divine absence are also well-attested aspects of the spiritual life. Even the greatest saints have been through periods of 'dryness', when God seems far away. This kind of 'desert' experience is not the same as unbelief, for it involves a holding on to the hidden God, even when tokens of the divine presence are not accessible. Retrospectively, such persistence is frequently seen to have been the source of spiritual growth. The most profound account of this kind of religious experience is St John of the Cross's description of the dark night of the soul, the forsaking of all consolations in the search for the reality of God alone.

Deception. Religious experiences of these kinds are in the highest degree personal. In such a subjective realm there is inevitably the possibility of vulnerability to illusion. To point this out, and to attempt the critical assessment that must accompany doing so, is by no means foreign to the Christian spiritual tradition. In fact, it is well recognized that religion is always in danger of demonic distortion, both at the communal level of the Church (crusades and persecutions) and at the individual level (visions and heavenly voices that invoke terrible deeds of destruction or, less traumatically, deceptive perceptions of personal significance and destiny). Hence the discipline of spiritual direction, the skills exercised by trained people to help others to recognize the true and to refuse the false. We find this need for discernment acknowledged in the New Testament: 'Beloved, do not believe every spirit, but test the spirits to see whether they are from God' (1 John 4.1).

Reason

The raw material for religious reflection is provided by Scripture and tradition (including the individual's own encounter with God and participation in the Christian community). Involved is not just a passive reception but also an active response. This will require not only obedience of conduct and discipline in worship, but also the exercise of the God-given gift of reason. Hence the quest for motivated belief that has been a constant theme in previous chapters, not least in connection with the insights of a revived and revised natural theology. The same stance carries over into the present task of theological reflection upon revelation. Indeed, the two activities of natural and revealed theology are simply dual aspects of the one theological quest for understanding. It is important, however, to have a clear sense of how reason can be expected to operate. Here some analogies with science can be helpful.

The history of quantum theory makes it plain that there is no universal epistemological method, nor a universal standard of rationality, which are known prior to our actual encounter with reality. Newtonian ideas had to be revised drastically in order to correspond with the idiosyncratic and totally unexpected character of the quantum world. The essence of rationality is to strive for conformity with the way things actually are found to be, discovered through the benign circularity of the interplay between interpretation and experience as they mutually influence each other.

A similar flexibility of reasonable response is also essential in theology as it engages with the realm of finite human experience of the infinite reality of God. Any procrustean attempt to impose prior patterns of interpretation will frustrate the search for theological understanding and prove to be the opposite of a rational intellectual strategy. A prime example will be provided by the discussion of the resurrection of Christ. A secular historian knows that people do not normally rise from the dead, but that cannot be permitted to conclude the discussion before it has begun, because it is precisely the Christian contention that here, in Jesus Christ, is an unprecedented situation to which normal experience will afford no adequate measure. The rational attitude is neither a sceptical dismissal nor a fideistic assertion, but a careful assessment of the evidence and its possible interpretation, both in relation to the alleged events and in relation to the wider coherence of meaning that might be attached to them. The circularity familiar from science is inevitably present here too: If Jesus is more than merely human, then it is possible that he was not held by death; if Jesus rose from the dead, then it is possible that he is more than merely human.

Jesus Christ: Resurrection

Much might be said about the figure of Jesus of Nazareth as he is presented to us in the Gospels: an authoritative preacher proclaiming the presence of the kingly rule of God, teaching and exemplifying a selfless love of others, catching the human imagination through parables which haunt the mind with their insistent questioning of conventional priorities, welcoming the outcasts of society into his company without compromising his own integrity, extending healing and compassion to those in need who cross his path. One should also add: a person who displays anger at the stubbornness of heart of those who turn away from the truth, someone who denounces hypocrisy and warns of judgement to come upon the city of Jerusalem, a man of hard sayings ('Let the dead bury their own dead', Matt. 8.22).

All these things make Jesus a significant figure, someone to be reckoned with, but they do not mark him off from other great religious figures, such as Moses, Mohammed and the Buddha. From the point of view of the history of religions, what is unique about Jesus is not his life but his death. All the other great religious founder-figures die in old age, surrounded by respectful disciples who will carry on the work and message of the

Master. Jesus, on the other hand, is executed in middle life, deserted by his disciples, an apparent total failure.

The Death of Christ

Crucifixion was a painful and usually lingering death, reserved by the Roman authorities for felons and rebellious slaves. Crucifixion was a death regarded with particular horror by a pious Jew because the verse in Deuteronomy (21.23), 'anyone hung on a tree is under God's curse', seemed to make it a sign of divine rejection. Crucifixion was the death that Jesus died. His followers, except for a few brave women, all ran away and Peter, their leader, was panicked into a threefold denial that he even knew Jesus. In the story of the garden of Gethsemane, the gospel writers tell us that Jesus faced this end with a mixture of acceptance and reluctance. From the darkness of the cross itself came the cry of dereliction, 'My God, my God, why have you forsaken me?', an utterance that was both so shattering and so significant that it had to be recorded also in Aramaic (Mark 15.34) or Hebrew (Matt. 27.46).

The death of Jesus is a profoundly ambiguous event. Is it the final extinction of a good man who, like so many good people both before and after him, was eventually beaten by the system? Is it the final act of a man of megalomaniac pretensions, trying to force the hand of God but eventually finding himself terribly mistaken? Is it just the kind of sad failure that happens all the time in this imperfect world?

From the very earliest times, the followers of Jesus have asserted that it is none of these things, but the cross is God's great act of reconciliation through Christ. Calvary is not the place of defeat but the place of victory and of hope for all humanity. In the intensely paradoxical and ironic words of St John's Gospel, the gallows was the throne on which God's Anointed One was 'lifted up'; the time of the crucifixion was the hour in which the Son of Man was glorified (John 12.23, 32). These astonishing assertions are possible because, from the very earliest times, the followers of Jesus believed that God had resolved the ambiguity of the crucifixion by raising Jesus from the dead. Death was not the end for him. On the truth or falsehood of that belief turns the whole Christian understanding of God and God's purposes in Jesus of Nazareth.

The Resurrection of Christ

Consideration of the credibility of the resurrection requires a twofold flow of argument. One stream is from below, looking at what historical reasons there might be to support such a counter-intuitive belief. The other stream is from above, looking to see whether the concept of Christ's resurrection can find some coherent place within what is otherwise believed about God's ways and purposes. 'Is there evidence?' and 'Does it make sense?', are the two basic questions to be addressed. We take the evidential question first.

Resurrection is not to be understood as a mere resuscitation, the restoring of life to a corpse destined to die again. Rather it is the transformation of one who has died into a new mode of glorified and everlasting life. The risen Christ is no longer confined by history, but his resurrection, nevertheless, may have left a deposit remaining within history. Search for evidence of that deposit involves a series of steps:

Something happened to turn the defeated and demoralized disciples of Good Friday into the confident proclaimers of the Lordship of Christ, just a few weeks later. Eventually many of them were to die for that belief. Whatever induced that transformation must have been of a magnitude commensurate with the total reversal of attitude that it produced.

The earliest account available to us of what that transforming event might have been is given in Paul's first letter to the Corinthians, where he recalls what he taught them when he founded their church, including the statement that Jesus 'was raised on the third day' (1 Cor. 15.4), adding to this a bare list of witnesses, most of them then still alive, who testified to having seen the risen Christ. Paul says that he 'handed on' to the Corinthians what he himself had received, presumably after his conversion on the road to Damascus which took place only a very few years after the crucifixion itself. Therefore this material originates very early indeed in the life of the Christian community, close to the events of which it claims to speak.

For accounts of what *the appearances of the risen Christ* might have been like, one must turn to the Gospels. There is considerable variation in detail and place present in these stories, in contrast to the broad agreement between the evangelists about the events leading up to the crucifixion. Nevertheless, there is also a common and unexpected theme present in the accounts, namely that it was not easy to recognize the risen Christ, the realization that it was indeed him coming in a moment of disclosure after initial failure to identify who it was. This surprisingly persistent pattern of delayed recognition can be seen as indicating the presence of a genuine historical reminiscence of what happened.

All four Gospels record, with differing minor details, the story of the discovery of *the empty tomb*, made by the women on the first Easter morning.

Since it was the common Roman custom to cast crucified bodies into an anonymous common grave, the authenticity of the story has been questioned. Yet Jewish polemic against the Christian claim of the resurrection (which can be traced back into the first century) always accepts that there was a tomb but proposes the (surely incredible) explanation that the disciples had deceitfully stolen the body.

Another possible source of doubt about the story lies in the absence of a clear reference to the empty tomb in Paul's writings (which predate the Gospels). Yet the brief account of 1 Corinthians 15 takes space to record of Jesus that he 'was buried', suggesting a significance attaching to this fact, and many think that a first-century Jew like Paul could not have believed that Jesus was alive (as Paul certainly did) while also believing that his body still lay mouldering in a tomb. Finally, if the tale were made up, why were women, unacceptable as legal witnesses in the ancient world, given the role of being the discoverers if not because that is what they actually were?

Certain aspects of *the life of the Church* add collateral support to the claim of the resurrection: the choice of the first day of the week to be the special Christian day (instead of the seventh day, the Jewish sabbath) seems anchored in the belief that it was the day of the Lord's rising; from New Testament times onwards, the characteristic Christian way of speaking of Christ has always been as a living contemporary and not as a revered founder-figure of the past.

Such lines of argument, briefly sketched here but capable of further elaboration, provide evidential motivation for belief in the resurrection. Without its having happened, it could be said, Jesus would never have been heard of after such a dismal end to his life. How one weighs that evidence, however, also depends upon the way our second question is to be answered. We have to go on to enquire, 'Does it all make sense?' A number of points can be made in response:

- It makes sense that God did not abandon the one person who wholly committed himself to the divine will, but God vindicated that person's faithfulness by delivering him from the grave.
- It makes sense that Jesus's life was not an ultimate failure but its culmination in the acceptance of the suffering of the cross brought ultimate victory over all the destructive powers that threaten human fulfilment.
- It makes sense that Jesus anticipates within history a destiny that awaits all other human beings beyond history. As Paul wrote to the

Corinthians, 'for as all die in Adam, so all will be made alive in Christ' (1 Cor. 15.22). The deep human intuition of hope, the defiance of mortality that is part of the human aspiration for fulfilment, finds its vindication in the anticipatory event of Jesus's resurrection. We shall return to this theme later in the chapter.

The resurrection of Christ is not something that can be established beyond a peradventure, or understood in a completely straightforward way. If it happened, it is the most significant event in all history and it carries with it profound implications for who Jesus really was. If it did not happen, Christianity is either deluded or reduced to a kind of pious wishing that it had been so. It is not easy to say precisely what 'happen' means for so unique an event, but its significance turns on the truth or falsehood of the fundamental Christian claim that 'Jesus lives!' No one can convince the sceptical against their will, but there is both significant historical and theological motivation for the belief. It is a belief held by the writer of this book.

Christology

If Jesus was not raised from the dead, he is a significant but tragic figure. If Jesus was raised from the dead, then he is a unique figure whose significance requires a great deal of further consideration. That further theological investigation is called Christology. Its pursuit starts in the pages of the New Testament. We shall begin with Paul.

New Testament Witnesses

The earliest Christian writing known to us is almost certainly Paul's first letter to the Thessalonians, most likely written in the year 50. He starts it with the greeting 'To the church of the Thessalonians in God the Father and the Lord Jesus Christ' (1.1). In one form or another this formula, bracketing God and Jesus, appears in the opening of almost all Paul's epistles. It is extremely odd for a monotheistic Jew to place a man, recently alive, alongside the God of Israel in this way. Moreover, Jesus is accorded the title 'Lord' (more than two hundred times in all in the Pauline writings), a word that carries with it distinct divine overtones, since pious Jews used it as an acceptable substitute for the unutterable divine name, YHWH, when reading aloud from scripture. Jesus is further spoken of as the one 'who rescues us from the wrath that is coming' (1.10); the one who is the ground of a hope of life beyond death since 'through Jesus, God will bring with him those who have died' (4.14);

human destiny is to be 'with the Lord for ever' (4.17). In later writings Paul will speak of Jesus as bringing a transforming power into believers' lives which is comparable to a 'new creation' (2 Cor. 5.17) or a new life (Rom. 6.11).

Expressed in various ways, one can find similar thoughts in the other New Testament writings, including the profound reflections on the significance of Jesus incorporated into the discourses of the Gospel according to St John. The predominant theme is that through his death and resurrection, Jesus has made available a new kind of life 'in Christ' and, in wrestling with this fact of their experience, these early Christian writers are driven to use more than simply human language about him. Yet these Jewish authors are also extremely reticent about saying out and out that Jesus is divine (a rare unambiguous statement to that effect is Thomas's confession in John 20.28, 'My Lord and my God!').

The Fathers of the Church

The matter could not be left in so unresolved a state. Exactly how did the Lordship of Christ relate to the Lordship of the God of Israel? Christological debate has continued throughout Christian history, but it was particularly intense in the first five centuries as the Fathers (the spiritual and intellectual leaders of the Church) struggled to find some coherent theological expression adequate to the Church's experience of its risen Lord. Many ideas were tried and rejected: adoptionism (a special man promoted to divine status at the resurrection – but if God was at work in Christ that had to be so from the very beginning); docetism (a heavenly figure who only appeared to be in human guise – but if Jesus was not a man how would he have any relevance to humanity?); Arianism (Jesus as a kind of intermediate figure located between God and humanity – but then he was identified with neither and so again became of doubtful relevance).

In the end, at the Council of Chalcedon in 451, a formula was adopted that was stronger at proscribing error than in articulating truth. Setting aside the subtleties of Greek philosophical language in which the Council's decision was expressed, we may say that the Chalcedonian Fathers asserted that divine language and human language were both indispensable in speaking of Christ and that neither should be subordinated to, or confused with, the other. It was like the physicists in the early years of the twentieth century, asserting that wavelike and particle-like language both belonged to light, without their being able to understand how this paradox might be resolved. There are times when one must cling to the strangeness of experience, resisting the temptation to deny part of that experience in order to achieve a facile, but unsatisfactory, relief from perplexity.

Contemporary Ideas

It is a task far beyond the scope of this book to attempt to survey Christological thinking over the centuries in any detail. Our main concern must be with the scientist-theologians, and others involved in the contemporary interaction between science and theology, who have offered some thoughts about this central Christian issue. Clearly it is well beyond the competency of science itself to pronounce on a unique life and its relevance to God and humanity. Scientific habits of thought, however, may have a contribution to make in this very different field of enquiry, not least through the 'bottom-up' approach of seeking understanding by moving from experience to interpretation. This is made the more likely by the fact, already noted, that Christological thinking first arose from the early church's wrestling with its experience of the phenomenon of the risen Christ and not from some kind of rash and unguarded metaphysical speculation about humanity and divinity in general. It is also possible that scientific ideas might provide an analogical resource for theology's engagement with Christological problems. Complementarity has already been suggested as a possibility, without at all claiming that ideas can be exported unproblematically from physics to theology.

The bottom-up thinker will first want to clarify what are the phenomena in need of explanation, for their character will control the plausibility of any explanation offered. In the case of Jesus Christ, one might derive from the New Testament the following criteria of Christological adequacy:

The Resurrection. Why was this man alone accorded victory over death within history, while the rest of humanity await that destiny beyond history?

Lordship. Within his lifetime and beyond it, Jesus claims and is accorded an authority that goes beyond what is appropriate to the merely human (e.g. in part of the Sermon on the Mount (Matt. 5), Jesus is portrayed as taking upon himself to add to and to deepen the divinely revealed *Torah* given to Moses at Sinai).

New Life. Christian testimony is that a transformed way of living is available to those who are 'in Christ' (the favourite Pauline expression is being part of 'the body of Christ' in a mysterious, super-personal way).

109

Universality. Jesus's death is said to be for the sins of the whole world. In a mysterious way, through his cross and resurrection, Jesus is the source of deliverance and new life for all people.

All Christian thought will want to give pre-eminence to Jesus Christ, if it is to be worthy of its name, but these New Testament accounts of what theologians call 'the work of Christ' (what he accomplished) set demanding conditions that an adequate Christological understanding will have to fulfil.

Two broad Christological strategies have been followed:

Functional Christology. This approach sees Jesus as realizing the full achievement of human potentiality and, through his fulfilment, being a person so fully aware of and open to the divine presence that he may be said to constitute 'a window into God'. The difference between Jesus and the rest of humanity is then a matter of degree, a supremely important matter of degree in which divine inspiration has played a significant part, but a matter of degree nevertheless. He became what we in principle might have become. Those who take this view frequently use evolutionary language to express their insight. Jesus is the 'new emergent', the latest development in the unfolding story of human potentiality. Jesus's uniqueness lies in his being the first person to have attained this degree of openness to God. In principle, it seems conceivable that eventually there might be others who do the same.

A functional Christology represents a way of assigning significance to Jesus in a manner that causes least difficulty or surprise in terms of ordinary understanding. Yet it has problems in meeting the criteria of Christological adequacy that have been identified above:

Resurrection and Lordship. The resurrection is an unprecedented event that does not seem in any way understandable as an intensification of previous partial experiences. If others do indeed 'emerge', will they too be resurrected within history? Will they also be accorded the title 'Lord' and be bracketed with God?

New Life and Universality. How does Jesus's emergence avail for us who have signally failed to emerge? The need of humanity seems to be for transforming power to lead the new life, much more than for an example of what that new life might be like.

Barbour has consistently espoused an evolutionary Christology of this functional kind. Perhaps it is significant that he has written little about the resurrection. Peacocke sometimes uses the concept of emergence, but his Christology also has in it elements of the second approach.

Ontological Christology. This approach is neo-Chalcedonian in that it seeks to hold to the mysterious, but exciting, idea that both human and divine language are used of Jesus Christ precisely because in him the life of humanity and the life of divinity are both actually present. The difficulty of the approach is clearly centred on what coherent meaning there could be in speaking of the combination of the finite and the infinite, the temporal and the eternal, the human and the divine. It could not be claimed that a clear exposition of this has been given, or even that such an achievement is likely to be possible for human thought. The motivation for the approach is that it seems to do best justice to the satisfaction of the New Testament criteria:

Resurrection and Lordship. Jesus died in solidarity with human mortality; he was raised from the dead by the power of God the Father in an act that is the seed of the work of new creation that God has begun in Christ. The resurrection is unique because the incarnation (humanity and divinity together in Jesus) is unique. Christ is bracketed with the Father and proclaimed Lord because of the divine dimension to his being.

New life and universality. Jesus Christ is the meeting place between the life of God and the life of humankind, the bridge by which Creator and creation are joined together. In the words of the Church Father Athanasius, 'He became human so that we might share in the life of God.' For this to be so, it is essential, as Chalcedon asserted, that Jesus is fully human (he is one of us) and fully divine (God is truly present in him and not just glimpsed through him).

Polkinghorne has consistently taken an ontological approach to Christology. He and Peacocke have both written about their understandings of the resurrection as event. Peacocke makes use of ontological concepts from time to time but it is not altogether clear how this relates to his employment also of the functional idea of emergence.

Orthodox Christology of this ontological kind makes profound assertions. It is not as readily accessible as the less mysterious functional Christology (just as quantum physics is less accessible than Newtonian physics) but it seems in better correspondence with the half-formed concepts used by the New Testament writers to describe their foundational experience of the Christ-event (a term used to refer to both pre-Easter and post-Easter encounters with Jesus). It is reasonable to expect conceptually demanding new ideas to demonstrate their value by exhibiting explanatory power beyond the phenomena that initially lead to their discovery. In the century of the Holocaust, the cross of Christ, understood in the way of an ontological account that sees God as actually present in that figure hanging on the tree, has given a deep insight into the suffering God. In the incarnate and crucified Christ, God is seen, not just as a compassionate spectator of the sufferings of creation, but as in truth a fellow participant, knowing these sufferings from the inside. This profound and moving thought has been classically expressed by Jürgen Moltmann in *The Crucified God*. Both Peacocke and Polkinghorne attach great importance to this Christian response to the problem of suffering.

The Trinity

While orthodox Christian thought ascribes divinity to Christ, no serious Christian theologian has ever simply equated Jesus to God. After all, as the Fathers often pointed out, he prayed to God throughout the course of his earthly life. Christ is called the Son of God in a strong ontological sense, but there is a distinction to be maintained between the Father and the Son. Matters became further complicated as the Church reflected upon its experience of the power of God at work in its midst and in the world. It spoke of this working as being due to God's Holy Spirit, drawing on language that had its origin in the Hebrew Scriptures. In the Old Testament, spirit is spoken of in rather impersonal terms, since it often seems to represent simply a particular power given to particular people (prophets, skilled craftsmen) for particular purposes. In the New Testament, however, a much more personal concept is involved, culminating in the remarkable passage in the letter to the Romans (8.22–7), where Paul speaks of the Spirit participating in the groaning and suffering of humanity and of all creation. If God deals with people as individuals, then God's Spirit must be subjective and personal (a 'Thou') and not just an objective and impersonal power (an 'it'). Considerations such as these led the Fathers, after much struggle, to reach the conclusion that, in the encounter with the divine, there was a meeting with the Holy Spirit, to be put in parallel with the meetings with the Father and the Son. By the fourth century, the distinctive Christian concept of the Trinity, the triune nature of God, had come to birth. The one God was also three 'Persons', Father, Son and Holy Spirit.

It is important to recognize that the doctrine of the Trinity arose 'from below', in an attempt to do theological justice to the actual character of the Church's encounter with God. Theologians call this experiential aspect the 'economic Trinity', how God is manifested in the *oeconomia*, the history of creation and the encounters of creatures with the divine. Trinitarian doctrine was not just a piece of rash metaphysical speculation, though attempts at its further elucidation sometimes led, perhaps inevitably, to less grounded conjectures about the 'essential Trinity', the divine nature in itself (sometimes also called the 'immanent Trinity'). These conjectures were expressed with all the subtlety of Greek philosophical thought, but they may be considered to have ventured beyond what could be expected to be within the grasp of finite minds.

Most theological thinking (indeed, one might say, most profound human thinking of any kind) is concerned with trying to steer a path between the errors that lie at the oversimplified extremes of a complex situation. In the case of the Trinity, one extreme was modalism, regarding the Persons as simply three perspectives on a single divine being, corresponding to three sorts of ways in which the One could be encountered (somewhat like the way one can encounter H_2O molecules as ice, water or steam). This seemed insufficiently to respect the distinctions which, for example, were represented by Jesus praying to the Father. The other extreme was tritheism, interpreting 'Person' in the modern sense of a separated centre of consciousness, and so creating a small Christian pantheon of three gods, in denial of the fundamental insight that Christianity had inherited from Israel that 'the Lord our God is one Lord' (Deut. 6.4).

Finding a middle way is not easy and it would not be possible to claim great theological success in the quest. For the purposes of this book, it is sufficient to note two important insights – both, it may be suggested, congenial to a scientist – which a substantial revival of Trinitarian discussion in recent years has placed on the contemporary theological agenda.

One is to recognize the relational nature of being. The doctrine of the Trinity offers the replacement of the classical Greek notion of the static being of God, frozen into immobility, so to speak, at the highest point of metaphysical eminence with nothing to do but contemplate the divine perfection (the God of Aristotle), by something altogether more dynamic, generated by the interchange of love between the Persons (technically, that mutual exchange and interpenetration that the theologians call *'perichoresis'*). Whatever the nature of the essential Trinity, it is surely relational. Modern science also encourages the use of relational concepts in its account of physical reality. The Newtonian picture of unchanging individual atoms colliding in the fixed container of pre-existing space has been replaced by Einstein's relativistic insight that space, time and matter are all interlinked, by quantum theory's togetherness-in-separation (the

EPR effect), and by the idea that all apparently individual electrons are actually excitations of energy in a common quantum field.

The second Trinitarian insight derives from the fact that the revived discussions have moved away from the kind of metaphysical speculations that were part of thinking in the later patristic period, turning back again to a closer linkage with experience. This modern attitude may be summed up by an aphorism of the Jesuit theologian, Karl Rahner, often called 'Rahner's rule': 'The economic Trinity is the essential Trinity.' God is known, not through soaring spiritual conjecture, but by the way in which God has actually chosen to make the divine nature known. One could paraphrase Rahner's rule by the critical realist slogan, 'Epistemology models ontology', what is known of God through experience of God is a sufficient guide to the divine nature.

Trinitarian theology is not some kind of mystical arithmetic in which it is decreed that $3 = 1$ but, rather, it is an insightful understanding of how God's activity in creation (the Father's holding of the universe in being), in redemption (the Son's sharing of humanity that we might share in divinity), and in sanctification (the transforming power of the Holy Spirit at work in human lives from within), come together as acts of the one true God, whose essence as Love is expressed in mutual interchange between the Persons of the Godhead.

Eschatology

One important implication of a theistic view of reality is that it assigns total meaningfulness to the universe and its history. The claim is that the world is truly a cosmos and not 'a tale told by an idiot'. This is because God's will and purpose, and God's assurance of an ultimate fulfilment, are behind all that is happening. The most obvious difficulty in substantiating this claim is the fact of death. Not only do all human lives come to a mortal end with much personal business and spiritual growth still unfinished and incomplete, but modern cosmology also assures us that the universe itself is condemned to die over a timescale of tens of billions of years.

Overall and all the time, the history of the universe has been a tug-of-war between two opposing tendencies: the expansive effect of the big bang, throwing matter apart; the contractive effect of gravity, pulling matter together. They are very evenly balanced and cosmologists cannot tell us which will win in the end. Therefore, there are two possible scenarios for future cosmic history. If expansion prevails, the galaxies will continue to fly apart for ever, condensing within themselves into gigantic black holes which eventually will decay into low-grade radiation. That way, the world ends with a whimper. If gravity prevails, the present galactic expansion will one day be halted and reversed, leading to collapse into the big crunch, as matter falls back into a cosmic melting pot. That way, the world ends with a bang. Either way, the universe, in terms of the extrapolation of its present history, is condemned to futility. This sobering thought led the distinguished theoretical physicist, Steven Weinberg, to say that the more he understood the universe, the more it seemed pointless.

Here is a challenge that theology has to face. Its response is called 'eschatology', the doctrine of the last things, the final end of present history. It is necessary to consider what can be said in the face of the fact of death, both about the destiny of individual human persons and about the destiny of the universe itself.

Human Destiny

In Chapter 3, it was suggested that the soul is the form, or immensely complex information-bearing pattern, of the body. That form is dissolved at death. In the purely naturalistic terms in which science has to speak, death then seems to be the end. In theological terms, however, only God is ultimate and if there is a human destiny beyond death, the hope of it resides in the faithfulness of a Creator who will not allow the creatures that are the subjects of the divine love simply to fall into nothingness. This is the point that Jesus made in his dispute with the Sadducees: the God of Abraham, Isaac and Jacob is 'God not of the dead, but of the living' (Mark 12.27). The patriarchs mattered to God in their earthly lives and so they matter to God for ever. It seems a coherent belief that God will remember and reconstitute the pattern that is a human being, in an act of resurrection taking place beyond present history. Thus the Christian hope centres on a real death followed by a real resurrection, brought about through the power and merciful faithfulness of God. Christianity is not concerned with a claim that there is human survival because there is an intrinsically immortal, purely spiritual, part in our being. The ground of hope for a destiny beyond death does not lie in human nature at all, but in divine, steadfast love. In Christian understanding, the paradigm for this eschatological destiny is the resurrection of Christ, the anticipation within history of what will happen to all others beyond history.

If human beings are psychosomatic unities, then the persons reconstituted in the divine act of resurrection must have new bodies to act as the carriers of the soul. It is not necessary, however, that the 'matter' of these bodies should be the same matter as makes up the flesh of this present world. In fact, it is essential that it should not be. That is because the material bodies of this world are intrinsically subject to mortality and decay. If the resurrected life is to be a true fulfilment, and not just a repeat of an ultimately futile history, the bodies of that world-to-come must be different, for they will be everlastingly redeemed from mortality. Science knows only the matter of this world but it cannot forbid theology to believe that God is capable of bringing about something totally new. However, theology must then explain, if the new creation is to be free from death and suffering, why God did not bring that world into being straight away, instead of the vale of tears of the old creation. Surely that would have been a better action?

Polkinghorne has suggested that the reason lies in the way in which the Creator's purposes require a two-step process; first a creation separate from God (allowed to make itself, as we thought theologically about an evolutionary universe), with the inevitable mortality that is the necessary cost of new life; then a new creation that is the transformation of the old and not its abolition, and which is not subject to mortality since it is no longer separated from God but integrated into the divine life ('theosis'). The old creation was created 'out of nothing'; the new creation is created 'out of the old'. That new creation lies beyond history, indeed it is the redemption of history, but Christians believe that the seed from which it has already begun to grow is the resurrection of Christ, an event both historical and eschatological in its character.

Cosmic Destiny

God must care for all creation, not just for human beings. Theology must, therefore, expect the universe also to have a destiny beyond its death. In fact, the 'matter' of the new creation, of which the preceding paragraph sought to speak, must be God's destiny for the futility-generating (entropy-increasing) matter of this world. We have already thought that the new creation arises 'out of the old' and not through a divine wiping of the cosmic slate clean for a second attempt at creation 'out of nothing'.

These are deeply mysterious thoughts, but they arise in theological discourse from the belief that existence makes total sense because God is ultimately steadfastly reliable, so that the universe is truly a cosmos and not the chaos that Weinberg feared it was destined to turn out to be. There are hints of this in the New Testament. In the letter to the Colossians, Paul speaks, most astonishingly, of the significance of Christ in truly cosmic terms: 'Through him [Christ] God was pleased to reconcile to himself all things [note, not just all people], whether on earth or in heaven [the known universe], by making peace through the blood of his cross' (1.20). Polkinghorne has emphasized that the empty tomb asserts that Christ's risen and glorified body is the transformation of his dead body, thereby implying a destiny in Christ for matter as well as for humanity.

There have been some scientists who have suggested that even within present physical process there might be a considerable degree of possible fulfilment. Carbon-based life is bound eventually to disappear from the universe as conditions become too hostile, but maybe 'intelligence' will engineer for itself further embodiments adapted to changing cosmic circumstances. The most ingenious, confident, and persistent of these 'physical eschatologists' has been Frank Tipler. He takes a highly reductionist view of life, equating it to information processing. If human beings are just computers made of meat then, when the meat can no longer exist, the programmes (which in Tipler's view are what life is) could be transferred to new types of hardware. Eventually, in the final collapse of a gravity-dominated universe, the whole cosmos might become an ever-faster racing computer, in its dying gasp processing an infinite amount of information. Tipler calls this hypothetical final cosmic state 'Omega' or a 'physical god'. He believes that Omega could 'resurrect' individuals by rerunning their 'programmes'. This extraordinary proposal is speculative to the highest degree (involving conjectures about the behaviour of states of matter totally beyond the reach of any reasonable extrapolation from current physical knowledge) and determinedly reductionist. It has not received wide acceptance.

Assimilation and Consonance

Tipler's stated intention is to make theology a branch of physics. Such an absorption of theology by science has been strongly resisted by the scientist-theologians, Barbour, Peacocke and Polkinghorne. The foregoing sketch of some of the issues in Christian thought should have made it plain that theology has its own domain in which evidence and concepts are operative that are specific to theological thinking and not reducible to something else. The personal and transpersonal experiences of religion are not to be equated with the mere epiphenomena of a fundamentally impersonal physical world. The eternal God, whose faithfulness is the ground of an everlasting hope, cannot be reduced to a transient cosmic supercomputer. Human destiny beyond death is not to be equated to split-second emulation in a realm of virtual reality.

Theology has a due autonomy that science must respect, in just the same way that science's deliberations are not open to theological control and interference. Yet knowledge is one and created reality is one (insights theologically underwritten by the unity of God) and so there must be some interrelationship between the insights and discourse of theology and the insights and discourse of science. The scientist-theologians all reject a 'two-languages', non-interactive account of the two disciplines. There remains the question of where, within the spectrum of relationship bounded by absorption at one end and total independence at the other, a balanced account of the interaction between science and theology is to be located.

One option might be called 'assimilation', the search for as close and accessible a conceptual relationship between the two subjects as can be achieved without the surrender of one to the other. Those who have followed this path have often made considerable use of evolutionary categories. Teilhard de Chardin's identification of his concept of Omega (to be distinguished from Tipler's) with both the goal of terrestrial evolution and with the coming of the Cosmic Christ, would be one example. Another would be the use of functional Christologies by people like Barbour. The concept of Jesus as the 'new emergent' is clearly intended to accord him significance without giving undue difficulty to secular comprehension, whatever problems there may be of its adequacy to the New Testament data. Process thought generally is assimilative in intention, despite the difficulties in reconciling it with science's account of physical process.

The second option might be called 'consonance'. It lays particular stress on theology's conceptual autonomy, but it recognizes that there must be a consistent fit with science where there is some degree of overlapping concern. Consonantists, like Polkinghorne, take an ontological view of Christology, since they believe that science is in no position to place constraints on how theology finds that it must understand this unique phenomenon, using terms that are adequate to the motivating evidence. In considering the doctrine of creation, however, theology must respect what science has to say about the evolving processes of the universe. These two examples bracket the range of a consonantist discussion. In between them lies the eschatological discussion of the previous section. Theology's expression of its hope must be consistent with science's prediction of physical futility, but theology is entitled to look beyond that and to make use of insights derived from its own conviction of the faithfulness of God.

Probably no one represents a pure case of these two strategies, but we have seen that there are approaches principally dependent on one or other stance. Peacocke's thought contains elements of both. Underlying the debate is the question of the degree of continuity with past tradition, and dependence upon past insight, that contemporary theologians need to acknowledge. Science is cumulative in the advance of its understanding. The average physics Ph.D. of today understands far more about the universe than even a genius like Sir Isaac Newton could ever have done in times past. Theology does not enjoy such monotonic progress. It is quite conceivable that thinkers of patristic or reformation times possessed understandings and spiritual perceptions not so readily accessible in our contemporary cultural setting. Theology can never dispense with the past, though it should not be in thrall to it either. Revisions are necessary (the Fall is an example, pp. 63–5), but so is respect for earlier ages. It is in the weighing of the balance between preservation and innovation in theological thinking, that much of the debate about assimilation and consonance is to be located.

7

The World Faiths

The second stage in the discussion of the interrelationships of the world faith traditions seeks to survey a truly ecumenical scene. It can only do so here in the broadest and most simplified terms. A sketch of the critical issues is the most that can be attempted. When one considers the slow rate of progress of ecumenical discussion within the Christian community of divided churches, it is clear that centuries of encounter are likely to be necessary before the world faiths make substantive progress in mutual dialogue.

The Sacred

Not all the traditions are even theistic, for Theravada Buddhism is at most agnostic, with the concept of nirvana said to play something like the fundamental role played by God in other faiths. Yet there is a common concern with a realm of spiritual significance and experience, however differently that realm is construed and described, that seems to link all the traditions in a common meeting with the sacred (understood as reality transcending the immediate and mundane). The similarity of reports of mystical encounters, in whatever tradition they occur, has already been noted and to a lesser extent the same is true of encounters with the numinous. When dedicated and serious followers of different faith traditions meet each other, they can often recognize the authenticity of the spiritual experiences of the other, despite the differences of linguistic expression that may be involved in their articulation.

The world faith traditions may be understood as preserving a testimony against a reductive, materialist account of reality. They hold out the prospect of some kind of fulfilment which is to be found in the spiritual realm. When one enquires more specifically about the character of that fulfilment, however, perplexing differences of description then become apparent.

120

Dissonance

Comparisons are complicated by the considerable differences present within each tradition itself, and also by the differing cultural settings in which each tradition finds its classic expression. Simplistic comparisons, such as the assertion that the Abrahamic faiths are world-affirming and the Eastern faiths world-denying, though crudely expressing actual differences of emphasis, run up against the tradition of the *Bhodisattvas* in Buddhism (enlightened ones who postpone their entry into nirvana in order to help others still in this world to find enlightenment in their turn) or the Desert Fathers in Christianity (whose extreme asceticism led to the rejection of the ordinary life of humankind). Cultural differences make the translation of the scriptures of the faiths an extremely delicate and difficult task, thereby increasing the problems of attaining mutual understanding. When all these caveats have been entered, it still seems possible to identify major points of disagreement between the traditions.

The human self. The Abrahamic faiths agree in assigning to individual human beings the highest significance in God's sight. Ancient Israel had a strong sense of the collective nature of the family and tribe (fathers and sons together, in the patriarchical language of the culture), but with the prophets of the Exile, such as Ezekiel, came the recognition of individual identity and responsibility and, later still, the expectation of a personal everlasting destiny beyond death. In the Gospels, Jesus is said to have asserted that such is God's care for the individual that the very hairs of our heads are numbered (Matt. 10.30).

The Eastern religions, on the other hand, and particularly Buddhism, see the self as ultimately an illusion from which to seek release, for clinging to individuality is the source of suffering. In contrast to Christianity's search for the purification that leads to right desire (the longing of the soul for God which is fundamental to the thought of Augustine), Buddhism's aim is the enlightenment that leads to non-desire.

The nature of time. Closely connected with the foregoing, there are differences in the attitudes to time that characterize the traditions. The Abrahamic faiths all have a strongly linear understanding of time, as a path to be trodden by the individual pilgrim. The Eastern faiths, on the other hand, see time in more circularly recurrent terms. This relates to the doctrine of reincarnation – so natural, it seems, to the Eastern mind, so perplexing to the Western. Those clinging to the illusion of self are destined to live a succession of lives as the wheel of *samsara* (reincarnation) revolves, until they find eventual release from this perpetual return.

Suffering. Within samsaric cyclicity, one's fate at the next turn of the wheel is determined by karma, the entail of good and evil carried forward from the past. This concept provides a ready-made, if unverifiable, explanation of the suffering to be endured in the present: it is the working out of bad karma, acquired in a previous life. For the Eastern religions, the problem of suffering is eventually solved by *anatta* (non-self) and the release from *samsara* that this brings.

For the Abrahamic faiths, suffering is a deadly reality and by no means the consequence of bondage to illusion. From the book of Job onwards, they have had to wrestle with the deep perplexities that this brings. A little of the Christian response has already been sketched (pp. 111–12), where insight is focused on the event of the cross of Christ.

History. A religion centred on the attainment of enlightenment is a religion whose principle concern is with timeless truths. It can sit light to history. Gandhi greatly valued Christ's teaching, such as in the Sermon on the Mount, but he said it was a matter of indifference to him whether Jesus had actually lived or not. Christianity is committed to the historical specificity of the life, death and resurrection of Jesus Christ, just as Judaism is committed to God's Passover deliverance out of Egypt and Islam to the life of Mohammed and the communication to him of the Qur'an. The Abrahamic faiths share a serious engagement with the reality of history, corresponding to their linear, progressive, understanding of the nature of time, within which their foundational revelatory events took place.

Monism. The Abrahamic faiths strongly emphasize the distinction between the Creator and creation. The universe is not divine. The Eastern traditions are monistic in their emphasis upon an ultimate unity of all reality, including the divine. In the advaitic tradition of Hindu thought, the Ultimate is *nirguna Brahman*, without any qualities, though religious practice makes the concession of speaking of *saguna Brahman*, reality with qualities. Monism underlines the assertion of the ultimate illusion of the self, for all are drops in the one ocean of being. This is an area in which the existence of different cultural and philosophical traditions, with the varieties of linguistic expression that go with them, enhances the danger of misunderstandings between the faiths, but it does seem that a fundamental dissonance is present.

Finally, one should note that, despite their commonalities, there are also serious dissonances within the family of Abrahamic faiths, not least in their assessments of Jesus of Nazareth. Islam regards him as one of the prophets, second only to Mohammed, and a number of contemporary Jews would wish to recognize him as an outstanding Jewish figure, though not the Messiah. Neither faith could accept the Christian belief in his divine status.

Responses

A variety of responses have been made to the clashing accounts of their encounters with the sacred, given by the world faiths.

Exclusivism

The classic Christian response was a simple assertion of the truth of Christianity and the error of religions that differed from it. In the early Christian centuries, the gods of other religions (other than the God of Israel, of course) were considered to be deceiving demons. In the nineteenth century, the same stance led an English missionary bishop in India to write a hymn speaking of how 'the heathen in his blindness bows down to wood and stone'. A principal motivation for this attitude arose from Christianity's claim of the unique and final character of God's self-revelation in Christ. In the often quoted words of Jesus in the fourth Gospel, 'No one comes to the Father except through me' (John 14.6). Yet the recognition of the authentic spiritual experience clearly contained in the other world faith traditions has made such a peremptory writing of them off an increasingly difficult position to maintain. After all, the fourth Gospel also speaks of the Word as 'the light of all people' (John 1.4).

Pluralism

This is the opposite stance, placing all faith traditions on an essentially equal footing. Of course, some limits are imposed, for adherents of this position are unlikely to be as accommodating to Satanism as to Judaism. Yet the major traditions of which we have been speaking are regarded as being equally valid, if culturally distinguishable, ways of attaining self-transcendence; and their accounts of deity, or the Ultimate, are seen as different masks behind which is hidden the ineffable Real. A great difficulty with this view is its mismatch with what the adherents of the

123

different faiths would want to say about their own understanding of the sacred. Such a bland commonality does not at all do justice to any tradition's specificities. It is very hard to believe that the dissonances noted in the previous section can be resolved in this way. The main motivation for pluralism is the belief that the Real cannot have been unknown and inaccessible for any enduring community. However, there can be other ways of attaining this desired conclusion.

Inclusivism

This is the stance favoured by many Christians who do not want to be dismissive of the spiritual experiences of their companions in other faiths, or to claim that they have nothing to learn from them, or to believe that God has left the divine nature altogether without witness at any time or place. Inclusivism, accordingly, does not deny the presence of genuine salvific experience in the different traditions, but neither does it deny the final and definitive character of God's self-revelation in Christ. Ultimately, all must indeed come to the Father through him, if he is the unique bridge between humanity and deity. But the light of the Word has also been shining in the other traditions, much as all Christians would acknowledge it to have shone in the Jewish faith. God is always and everywhere at work (through the hidden activity of the Spirit) and no community has been without some degree of true encounter with the divine. Karl Rahner was aiming at an inclusivist statement when he called the adherents of other faiths 'anonymous Christians'. Of course, they might well wish to repudiate a description that might seem to them to amount to a Christian takeover bid, but Rahner was trying to speak of comradeship rather than annexation. Like many theological positions, inclusivism is more a statement of the boundaries within which an acceptable solution may be sought, rather than the attainment of that solution. The perplexities of dissonance still remain to be resolved.

Continuing Discussion

There is clearly a correlation between these attitudes to interfaith matters and the understandings of the theological enterprise that were discussed in Chapter 1. Those taking a cognitive approach will incline to exclusivism, for propositions are either true or false. Both the experiential-expressive and cultural-linguistic approaches seem hospitable to forms of pluralism and, in fact, a desire to attain some kind of ecumenical coexistence has been a factor in encouraging these ways of conceiving of theological discourse. If religion is fundamentally about inner attitudes or patterns of community living, then one must expect much cultural variety and, indeed, encourage it, for what suits one person or society will not necessarily suit another. The considerable diversities within each faith tradition are clearly accommodating human variety in this way. However, if there is also a cognitive element within religion, a concern with what is actually the case, then the problems of dissonance remain.

Inclusivism is naturally allied to a critical realist understanding of theology: acknowledging the universal presence of encounter with the sacred; seeking to understand its different modes of expression and description, while recognizing that each tradition and community must view reality from a cultural perspective; knowing that interpretation and experience intertwine, yet believing that behind it all is an actual Reality of which we may hope to gain verisimilitudinous understanding; trusting that this Reality is such that an understanding of it is, at least to some degree, attainable by humankind.

There is a growing feeling that none of the classic interfaith approaches of exclusivism, pluralism or inclusivism, in terms of their simple categorizations, are adequate to the complexity and perplexity of the meeting of the world faith traditions. This truly ecumenical dialogue is still at a very early stage. In the concluding section, we shall consider a way in which a further small advance might be made.

Science as a Meeting Point

Each world faith is the jealous guardian of its central tenets and its fundamental style of discourse. Even Hinduism, the most accepting of the traditions in terms of accretions from elsewhere, sets limits to its tolerance by the rejection of what it sees as intolerably exclusive claims. Jesus can be welcomed as an *avatar* (one of a number of appearances of the divine in human form) but not accepted as the only-begotten Son of God. Initial dialogue between the traditions will have to take place at their peripheries, for encounter at the centre would be too threatening.

It is possible that the consideration of the relationship between scientific and religious understandings would provide a place of meeting where meaningful issues could be raised without inducing a merely defensive response. A great deal of the material of Chapters 1 to 5 would be suitable for reconsideration in this ecumenical way, but only through discussions between a number of adherents of the different faiths who also shared a concern for these questions arising from science. Any single author (including, of course, the present one) cannot step far outside the world of meaning within which his or her scientific and religious experience has been realized. No one can pretend to attain some magisterial vantage point from which neutral adjudication could be given. We can listen to each other, but we cannot presume to speak for each other.

Some of the questions that would be included in the agenda for such a meeting would be:

- How do we understand the nature of the physical world and our relationship to it? What is the kind of knowledge we can attain? What is the meaning of the Eastern concept of *maya*, often understood by occidentals as asserting that we live in a world subject to the play of illusion?

- What is the relationship between religious metaphysics and quantum theory's mixture of structure and flexibility and its picture of an interconnected web of events which participate in togetherness-in-separation? Do indigenous adherents of Hinduism and Buddhism detect the same resonant correspondences that some Western writers have claimed to exist between quantum theory and Eastern thought?

- How do a cosmic evolutionary history stretching over fifteen billion years and a biological evolutionary history stretching over four billion years relate to the creation stories of the faith traditions?

- Are the deep intelligibility of the physical world, and the 'unreasonable effectiveness of mathematics' in its scientific description, signs of the cosmic presence of Mind?

- Is the anthropic fine tuning of the laws of nature in this universe a sign of the cosmic presence of Purpose?

- How do the insights of neurophysiology, psychology and the philosophy of the mind affect our understanding of the human person? Is there a coherent and stable concept of the human self?

- What is the significance of science's prediction of eventual cosmic collapse or decay?

- Does analogy with the scientific community offer any insight into the balance within the religious life between cognitive understanding, expressive commitment and a communally conducted life?

- What role does bottom-up thinking, so natural to the scientist in the way it seeks to move from evidence to understanding, have to play in the intellectual reflection upon religious claims?

It is earnestly to be hoped that a conversation of this kind will come about. It may be expected to continue for a very long time. Bottom-up thinkers would welcome the start of conversations focused on these specific issues, for not everything that needs to be done in the ecumenical encounter of the world faith traditions can be achieved through the top-down discussion of general principles.

8

The Search for Knowledge
and Wisdom

At the conclusion of our discussion, it is appropriate to try to set the interaction between science and theology in a wider context.

The Two Disciplines

Science is part of human culture and in its turn it influences that culture, but its controlling factor is its encounter with the reality of the physical world. Theology is also part of human culture. It too is both influenced by general culture and also exerts a responsive influence upon that culture, but its controlling factor is its encounter with the reality of God. The quest for true understanding, seeking to attain knowledge through motivated belief, is what the two disciplines have in common. There are, however, two striking differences between them.

One lies in the nature of their controlling factors. Human beings transcend the physical world and can put it to the experimental test. God transcends humanity and is not to be put to the test by any creature. Science and theology lie at the opposite ends of a spectrum of rational human enquiry into reality. At the scientific end is the realm of impersonal experience; at the theological end is the realm of the experience of the transpersonal. In between lie the realms of human personal encounter with reality, which are the subjects of disciplines such as aesthetics and ethics. The whole spectrum of enquiry makes up the rich many-stranded texture of human knowledge, surveying the encounter with the multi-levelled reality of the one world of human experience. Ultimately, all these insightful disciplines must find their mutual reconciliation and integration with each other. The discussion of the interaction of science and theology is but a part of that single search for unified understanding.

The second difference also relates to the impersonal/transpersonal contrast, but it concerns the consequences of belief rather than the content of belief. In Chapter 1, we rejected the pragmatic account of the nature of science, but it is certainly the case that scientific under-standing enables people to get things done. Science's offspring is technol-ogy. One has only to think of atomic energy, information technology and genetic engineering to see how vastly science has enhanced the portfolio of possible human interventions in nature. Science provides opportunities for action, but it does not itself tell us how these opportunities should be used. It confers knowledge but not wisdom.

In religion, however, belief is inseparable from praxis, for a religious understanding carries unavoidable implications for conduct. Morality can be distinguished from religion (as the humane integrity of atheists' ethical behaviour makes clear), but there is an inevitable moral component to the religious life. Jesus said, 'You will know them by their fruits' (Matt. 7.20). While in Chapter 1 we rejected a purely experiential-expressive account of theological discourse, those who assert that God is love are called to live a correspondingly agapeistic life. 'Those who say, "I love God", and hate their brothers or sisters, are liars' (1 John 4.20). Theology seeks to confer not only knowledge of the divine will but also the wisdom to make right choices and to live lives conformed to God's good and perfect will.

Ethical Issues

This book has principally dealt with intellectual questions, but a significant part of the actual interaction between the scientific and theological communities is concerned with questions of ethical choice. In conclusion, brief consideration will be given to some of the broad principles involved in this exchange. Their full discussion, including the necessary consideration of case histories and specific problems, would require another volume.

Limits

Science is very exciting; the scent of discovery quickens the intellectual appetite. Technology is very beguiling; if something can be done, why not go ahead and do it? It is necessary to ask the question of whether scientific and technological activities are without bounds, or are there limits that should be set to them?

In terms of methods to be employed, there is wide acknowledgement that there are ethical constraints that may not be set aside. Experiments on human patients without informed consent and without primary concern for the benefit of the individual patient involved might advance medical knowledge, but they are unacceptable to medical ethics. Those who believe that experiments on live animals are permissible only allow them subject to stringent safeguards. The seriousness of the scientific aim (arising above mere curiosity) and the control and minimization of the pain produced, together with a proportionality between human gain and animal loss, are important factors to be taken into account in deciding whether a particular experiment should be permitted.

The means, then, must be ethical, but what about the ends? In relation to what are permissible aims and achievements of scientific research, there is greater scope for discussion and greater scope for disagreement. Not everything that can be done should necessarily be done. The technological imperative ('Come on, we can do it; let's do it') must be tempered by the moral imperative ('Are the means and ends involved ethically acceptable?'). In evaluating these issues, a distinction can be drawn between science and technology.

Science is concerned with the advance of knowledge. Not only is it difficult practically to set limits to this advance (for if the discovery is not made in laboratory A, then laboratory B, hot on the same track, is likely to make it instead) but it is open to argument that the increase of knowledge is in itself inherently desirable. Surely, knowledge is a better basis for decision than ignorance. In order to make a right decision, of course, wisdom must be added to knowledge, but we have argued that wisdom is outside science's own self-limited domain of competence and so it must be sought elsewhere. Against this endorsement of the desirability of intellectual progress, people have sometimes argued that there are intrinsically undesirable forms of knowledge. For example, it has been suggested that if there are genetic causes that produce differences of average physical strength or average mental ability between different racial groups, it would be better not to know this, lest the knowledge led to unfair stereotyping.

Technology is concerned with getting things done and it is in relation to its consequences that ethical issues seem most clearly to arise, putting the question of limits firmly on to the moral agenda. Manipulation of the human genome could lead to the elimination of certain types of serious congenital disease, but currently there is an agreed limitation that does not permit germ-line therapy (that is, intervention in genetic material that could transmit consequences to future generations, as compared to somatic gene therapy which seeks to repair defective genes in the individual without producing future consequences beyond that individual). This moratorium has been imposed partly because of anxieties about the safety of germ-line therapy, since long-term consequences are very hard to predict, but also partly because there are some who accept an intuition that the stuff of human life carries a moral value that prohibits tampering with it. Similar considerations have limited *in vitro* experiments on fertilized human embryos to the fourteen-day period before the appearance of the primitive streak (understood as the sign of the onset of cell differentiation). There are a variety of religious assessments of the moral status of the early unimplanted embryo, but there is a widely held recognition that it is entitled to profound ethical respect as possessing, at the least, potentiality for human life. The scientific and technological community has shown that it recognizes that not everything that can be done should be done.

The Role of Experts

The advice of experts is indispensable in the search for wise decisions about technological projects. Only they are in a position to evaluate the potential advantages and disadvantages of new developments. Experts have an ethical obligation to offer this advice in as fair and scrupulous a way as possible, neither concealing problems nor exaggerating benefits. The general public has an obligation to pay attention to the advice of the experts, provided they are satisfied that it is being tendered in a sober and responsible manner. Yet the experts cannot be left to be judges in their own cause. They are not necessarily exceptionally wise as well as being exceptionally knowledgeable. Inevitably, they view the issues from their own perspective and the excitement of scientific and technical advance can impose its own distortion on ethical judgement, or distraction from it. Experts must be prepared to be in serious dialogue with the general public and to consider its question whether some particular new thing that is possible should actually be done.

The Los Alamos project for building the first atomic bomb probably represented the greatest concentration of scientific talent ever assembled for a common purpose. The problems involved in design and construction were greatly challenging. The project's scientific director, Robert Oppenheimer, said that the science was 'very sweet'. Many of the leaders of that great enterprise subsequently wrote their memoirs of life on that mesa in New Mexico. It was an isolated and self-contained community, for security reasons as well as because of its geographical location. It is something of a shock, nevertheless, to gather the impression that many of these highly intelligent people only began seriously to ask themselves what it was that they were doing when they saw the first test explosion in the New Mexico desert, well past the point of no return as far as exploitation was concerned. This is not the place to argue the pros and cons of the atomic bomb project itself, but surely ethical matters

131

should have been taken into account by the experts at an earlier stage. The technological imperative seems to have eclipsed the moral imperative.

The best hope of wise moral decisions lies in encouraging dialogue between the experts and the public in general at as early a stage as possible, preferably before the technology is on the shelf ready for use. Society needs to create meeting places in which such discussions can take place in a careful and realistic way. The clash of single-issue pressure groups, one claiming that X is the best thing ever, the other that X is the worst thing ever, is unlikely to lead to wise conclusions, for in virtually every advance there is a balance of potential gain and potential loss that requires responsible ethical evaluation.

Integrity of Nature

Science is increasingly aware of the intricate and interrelated character of the world. Delicate, and only partly understood, self-regulating mechanisms have kept the oxygen content of the Earth's atmosphere and the salinity of its seas pretty well constant for hundreds of millions of years, despite variations in other circumstances that might have been expected to be disrupting. Ecological systems involve complex symbiotic relationships between flora and fauna in mutually sustaining connections. Disturbing these equilibria, whether by introducing rabbits into Australia or releasing fluorocarbon sprays into the atmosphere, can have severe consequences that only become apparent after the initiating event and which are then often very difficult to reverse. It is increasingly recognized that there is an ethical duty of care due to the life-sustaining systems of Earth, a necessary respect for the integrity of nature.

Considerable subtlety is involved, however, in understanding what constitutes the integrity of nature. It certainly is not a total absence of change, which is impossible in an evolutionary world. Times of the depletion of life have also been times of genetic progression. It was the ecological disaster of a meteorite impact sixty-five million years ago that destroyed the dinosaurs and gave the little furry mammals that were our ancestors their evolutionary opportunity. Presently, human intervention in nature is eliminating species at ten thousand times the normal rate. We cannot feel complacent about such a haemorrhage of biodiversity, but the preservation of every species cannot be made an absolute requirement either. We also have natural enemies. Who can lament the elimination of the smallpox virus?

The Ground of Ethics

Two broad guidelines that are often applied to the ethical discussion of the exploitation of science and technology are that the resulting use should be just and sustainable.

'Just' refers to a contemporary obligation to respect the common good. It implies that there should be a fairness in sharing, so that no one group of nations (North over South), or class of society (rich over poor), takes an excessive share of the benefit, with the result that it is then denied to the others. The 'green revolution' that has greatly enhanced the total fertility of the Earth should result in food for all, satisfying the needs of the primary producers as well as the needs of the consumer nations.

'Sustainable' refers to a future obligation to respect the needs of generations yet unborn. The Earth's non-renewable resources (such as fossil fuels and minerals) are not to be squandered in gratifying current conspicuous consumption, but they should be conserved as much as possible in order to provide for those who will come after us, as well as for ourselves. For this reason there is a degree of ethical obligation to encourage research into the viable exploitation of renewable energy sources (such as wind and wave power).

Many people of ethical good will, whether of religious belief or not, would accept these two guiding principles. The religious believer, in addition, can offer a ground for their adoption which explains the origin of these moral intuitions. The Earth's resources are not there to be grasped for our present satisfaction, heedless of the needs of others present or future, because the Earth itself is not ours but God's. We are creatures who receive nothing that is not given to us. Creation exists solely because of divine generosity, for creatures to share and to enjoy and to hand on. Human beings are the stewards of terrestrial creation, not its owners. A most significant aspect of the interaction between science and theology is the latter's provision of a ground for the ethical guidelines within which the great endeavour of science and technology can only rightly be pursued.

Bibliography

General

Three major authors are scientists who have turned their attention to theological issues, the scientist-theologians: Ian Barbour, Arthur Peacocke, John Polkinghorne. Frequent reference will be made to their work in what follows and their principal writings are accordingly abbreviated as shown:

I.G. Barbour:
ISR: *Issues in Science and Religion* (SCM Press, 1966).
MMP: *Myths, Models and Paradigms* (SCM Press, 1974).
RAS: *Religion in an Age of Science* (SCM Press, 1990).

A.R. Peacocke
CWS: *Creation and the World of Science* (Oxford University Press, 1979).
IR: *Intimations of Reality* (University of Notre Dame Press, 1984).
GNB: *God and the New Biology* (Dent, 1986).
TSA: *Theology for a Scientific Age* (enlarged edition, SCM Press, 1993).

J.C. Polkinghorne
OW: *One World* (SPCK/Princeton University Press, 1986).
SC: *Science and Creation* (SPCK/Shambhala, 1988).
SP: *Science and Providence* (SPCK/Shambhala, 1989).
RR: *Reason and Reality* (SPCK/Trinity Press International, 1991).
SCB: *Science and Christian Belief/The Faith of a Physicist* (SPCK/Princeton University Press, 1994).
ST: *Scientists as Theologians* (SPCK, 1996).
BS: *Beyond Science* (Cambridge University Press, 1996).
BG: *Belief in God in a Scientific Age* (Yale University Press, 1998).

ST is devoted to a comparison of the writings of these three scientist-theologians.

Seven other general books, each with a distinctive approach, are:

W.B. Drees, *Religion, Science and Naturalism* (Cambridge University Press, 1996). A closely argued presentation combining an exclusively naturalistic account of phenomena with theistic answers to certain 'limit questions'.

J.F. Haught, *Science and Religion* (Paulist Press, 1995). A number of questions are raised, to each of which four contrasting responses are offered, corresponding to stances characterized as embodying conflict, contrast, contact and confirmation, respectively.

P. Hefner, *The Human Factor* (Fortress, 1993). A discussion set in a broad, humane, cultural context and making substantial appeal to evolutionary insights. A key concept is of human beings seen as 'created co-creators' with God.

N. Murphy and G.F.R. Ellis, *On the Moral Nature of the Universe* (Fortress, 1996). Particular attention is paid to the social sciences, seen as undergirded by ethical considerations, and to the role of value in framing a general cosmology.

W.M. Richardson and W.J. Wildman, eds., *Religion and Science* (Routledge, 1996). A well-edited volume in which the discussion of historical and methodological questions is followed by six case studies in each of which two authors (a scientist and a theologian) explore an issue of contemporary significance.

H. Rolston, *Science and Religion* (Temple University Press, 1987). Particular attention is paid to ecological issues and the discussion includes the social sciences as well as the natural sciences.

M.W. Worthing, *God, Creation and Contemporary Physics* (Fortress, 1996). A book that concentrates on a detailed discussion of issues arising from contemporary physics, especially quantum theory and cosmology.

Finally, one may note books by theologians who display sympathy to the need to take science seriously:

W. Pannenberg, *Towards a Theology of Nature*, ed. T. Peters (Westminster/John Knox Press, 1993).

T.F. Torrance, *Theological Science* (Oxford University Press, 1969). Difficult, but important.

1   The Area of Interaction

Discussions of the philosophy of science, the nature of theology, and comparisons and interactions between the two, can be found in *BG*, Chs 2, 5; *CWS*, Ch 1; *IR*; *ISR*, Chs 6, 8, 9, *MMP*; *OW*, Chs 2, 3; *RAS*, Ch 1–3; *RR*, Chs 1, 2, 4; *SC*, Ch 6; *SCB*, Ch 2; *ST*, Ch 2; *TSA*, Introduction.

J.H. Brooke, *Science and Religion* (Cambridge University Press, 1991). An excellent survey of historical issues (together with a detailed bibliography).

S. Jaki, *Science and Creation* (Scottish Academic Press, 1986). A scholarly argument that Christian thought provided the matrix for the birth of modern science.

C. Kaiser, *Creation and the History of Science* (Marshall-Pickering, 1991). A scholarly and detailed historical account of what the author calls 'the creationist tradition' (not at all the same as contemporary creationism).

J. Leplin, ed., *Scientific Realism* (University of California Press, 1984). A variety of contributions, both criticizing and supporting critical realism.

G.A. Lindbeck, *The Nature of Doctrine* (SPCK, 1984). A presentation of Lindbeck's ideas.

N. Murphy, *Theology in the Age of Scientific Reasoning* (Cornell University Press, 1990). A Lakatosian approach to theology.

W.H. Newton-Smith, *The Rationality of Science* (Routledge & Kegan Paul, 1981). A critical survey of twentieth-century philosophy of science.

M. Polanyi, *Personal Knowledge* (Routledge & Kegan Paul, 1958).

D. Scott, *Michael Polanyi* (SPCK, 1996). An accessible discussion of Polanyi's thought.

J.M. Soskice, *Metaphor and Religious Language* (Oxford University Press, 1985). A careful discussion of the role of metaphor.

2 The Scientific Picture of the World

Discussion of quantum issues can be found in *RAS*, Ch 4; *RR*, Ch 7; of cosmology in *RAS*, Ch 5; *SCB*, Ch 4; of evolution (mainly biological) in *CWS*, Chs 2, 3; *GNB*, Chs 5, 6; *RAS*, Ch 6; of chaos and complexity in *TSA*, Ch 3; *SC*, Ch 3; *RR*, Ch 3.

J.D. Barrow and F.J. Tipler, *The Anthropic Cosmological Principle* (Oxford University Press, 1986. An encyclopedic account of all matters relating to the Anthropic Principle.

P.W. Davies, *The Cosmic Blueprint* (Heinemann, 1987). An assessment of the cosmic drive to complexity.

P.W. Davies, *About Time* (Viking, 1995). A wide-ranging discussion of ideas about time, including some that are speculative.

B. d'Espagnat, *Reality and the Physicist* (Cambridge University Press, 1989). A sophisticated philosophical discussion of quantum theory.

W. Drees, *Beyond the Big Bang* (Open Court, 1990). A critical account of cosmological theories and their possible theological significance.

J. Gleick, *Chaos* (Heinemann, 1988). A popular account of chaos theory.

C.J. Isham, 'Quantum Theories of the Creation of the Universe', in R.J. Russell, N. Murphy and C. J. Isham (eds.), *Quantum Cosmology and the Laws of Nature* (Vatican Observatory, 1993). An introduction to quantum cosmology.

C.J. Isham and J.C. Polkinghorne, 'The Debate over the Block Universe' in Russell et al., *Quantum Cosmology*. A debate of the pros and cons of the block universe.

S. Kauffman, *At Home in the Universe* (Viking, 1995), Kauffman's ideas.

J. Leslie, *Universes* (Routledge, 1989). A concise but full and very readable account of the Anthropic Principle.

J.C. Polkinghorne, *The Quantum World* (Penguin, 1990). Useful conceptual introduction to quantum theory.

I. Prigogine, *The End of Certainty* (The Free Press, 1997). An interpretation of dynamical theory as open to the future.

I. Prigogine and I. Stengers, *Order out of Chaos* (Heinemann, 1984). On dissipative systems.

A. Rae, *Quantum Physics: Illusion or Reality?* (Cambridge University Press, 1986). Useful conceptual introduction to quantum theory.

M. Rees, *Before the Beginning* (Simon & Schuster, 1977). An up-to-date account of cosmology, carefully distinguishing well-established ideas from more speculative thinking.

D. Ruelle, *Chance and Chaos* (Princeton University Press, 1991). A mathematical account of chaos theory.

I. Stewart, *Does God Play Dice?* (Blackwell, 1989). A mathematical account of chaos theory.

3 Humanity

Further discussions of reductionism can be found in: *CWS*, Ch 4; *GNB*, Ch 1; *OW*, Ch 6; *RAS*, Ch 6; of human nature in *RAS*, Ch 7; *SCB*, Ch 1; *TSA*, Chs 4, 12; of the philosophy of mind in *BS*, Ch 5; of the Fall in *RR*, Ch 8; *TSA*, pp. 242–3, 248–9.

J. Bowker, *Is God a Virus?* (SPCK, 1995). A critique of genetic reductionism.

J.B. Cobb and D.R. Griffin, *Process Theology* (Westminster Press, 1976). Introduction to both process philosophy and process theology.

F. Crick, *The Astonishing Hypothesis* (Simon & Schuster, 1994). Physicalist approach to the question of mind.

R. Dawkins, *The Selfish Gene* (Oxford University Press, 1976). Genetic reductionism is expounded in this and subsequent writings.

D.C. Dennett, *Consciousness Explained* (Little, Brown, 1991). Physicalist approach to the question of mind.

J. Eccles, *The Human Mystery* (Routledge & Kegan Paul, 1984). A defence of dualism by a Nobel-prizewinning neurophysiologist.

D. Hodgson, *The Mind Matters* (Oxford University Press, 1991). An attempt to tackle the mind/body problem using quantum theory.

M.A. Jeeves, *Human Nature at the Millennium* (Appolos, 1997). A discussion of how modern neuropsychology and biblical anthropology relate to each other.

M. Lockwood, *Mind, Brain and the Quantum* (Blackwell, 1989). An attempt to tackle the mind/body problem using quantum theory.

T. Nagel, *The View from Nowhere* (Oxford University Press, 1986). Philosophy sympathetic to dual-aspect monism.

D. Parfitt, *Reasons and Persons* (Oxford University Press, 1944), Chs 10–15. Difficulties felt by a philosopher about the concept of personal identity.

R. Penrose, *The Emperor's New Mind* (Oxford University Press, 1989). Includes an attempt to tackle the mind/body problem using quantum theory.

R. Penrose, *The Shadows of the Mind* (Oxford University Press, 1994). Penrose replies to his critics.

J.R. Searle, *The Rediscovery of Mind* (MIT Press, 1992). Includes a defence of folk psychology and an emergentist approach.

A.N. Whitehead, *Process and Reality* (The Free Press, corrected edition, 1978). The classic source of process thinking.

4   Theism

Discussion of the divine nature can be found in *RAS*, Ch 9; *SCB*, Ch 3; *TSA*, Chs 6–8; of natural theology in *BG*, Ch 1; *RR*, Ch 6; *SC*, Chs 1, 2; of evolution and continuing creation in *CWS*, Chs 2, 3; *GNB*, Chs 5–7; *ISR*, Ch 12, *RAS*, Ch 6; *SC*, Ch 4; *SCB*, Ch 4.

J. Begbie, *Voicing Creation's Praise* (T. & T. Clark, 1991). The relation between art and theology.

P. Berger, *A Rumour of Angels* (Penguin, 1970). 'Signals of transcendence' are discussed.

B. Davies, *The Thought of Thomas Aquinas* (Oxford University Press, 1992). A useful introduction to the thought of Thomas Aquinas.

P.C.W. Davies, *God and the New Physics* (Dent, 1983). Natural theology developed outside a religious tradition.

P.C.W. Davies, *The Mind of God* (Simon & Schuster, 1992). Further thoughts on natural theology developed outside a religious tradition.

R. Dawkins, *The Blind Watchmaker* (Longman, 1986). A biologist asserts the meaninglessness of evolutionary history.

C. de Duve, *Vital Dust* (Basic Books, 1995). An optimistic assessment of the ease with which life might originate.

D.C. Dennett, *Darwin's Dangerous Idea* (Simon & Schuster, 1995). A claim that Darwinian ideas explain practically everything.

J. Monod, *Chance and Necessity* (Collins, 1972). A biologist asserts the meaninglessness of evolutionary history.

G. Steiner, *Real Presences* (Faber & Faber, 1989). The relation between art and theology.

R. Swinburne, *The Existence of God* (Oxford University Press, 1979). An early work developing particular aspects of his philosophical approach to theistic belief.

R. Swinburne, *Is There a God?* (Oxford University Press, 1996). An accessible summary of Swinburne's philosophical approach to theistic belief.

5   Divine Action

Discussion of divine action can be found in *BG*, Ch 3; *IR*, Ch 2; *RAS*, Ch 8; *RR*, Ch 3; *SCB*, Ch 4; *SP*, Chs 1–4; *ST*, Ch 3; *TSA*, Chs 9, 11; of God's relation to time in *SP*, Ch 7; of theodicy in *RAS*, Ch 9; *SC*, Ch 4; *SP*, Ch 5.

J. Bowker, *Licensed Insanities* (Darton, Longman & Todd, 1987), Appendix. A general account of God as acting through information input.

J. Hick, *Evil and the God of Love* (Macmillan, 1966). A useful survey of various approaches to the problem of evil.

G.M. Jantzen, *God's World, God's Body* (Darton, Longman & Todd, 1984). A defence of the idea of divine embodiment.

G.D. Kaufman, *God the Problem* (Harvard University Press, 1972). A single action account of divine action.

J. Moltmann, *The Trinity and the Kingdom of God* (SCM Press, 1981), Ch 4. Among Moltmann's work, this particularly emphasizes the divine 'making way' to allow ontological space for creation.

J. Moltmann, *God in Creation* (SCM Press, 1985), Ch 4. This too emphasizes the divine 'making way' to allow ontological space for creation.

R.J. Russell, N. Murphy and A.R. Peacocke (eds.), *Chaos and Complexity* (Vatican Observatory, 1995). A variety of contrasting approaches to divine action.

W.H. Vanstone, *Love's Endeavour, Love's Expense* (Darton, Longman & Todd, 1977). A sensitive account of the inherent precariousness of creativity by Love.

K. Ward, *Divine Action* (Collins, 1990). A theological discussion of many aspects of divine action.

K. Ward, *Rational Theology and the Creativity of God* (Blackwell, 1982). A dipolar account of deity very different from that of process theology.

V. White, *The Fall of the Sparrow* (Paternoster Press, 1985). A discussion of God's agency, framed in terms of tight divine control.

M.F. Wiles, *God's Action in the World* (SCM Press, 1986). A single action account of divine action.

6   Christian Theology

Discussion of the nature of revelation, Scripture and related topics can be found in *MMP*, Chs 4, 7; *RR*, Ch 5; *SCB*, pp. 33–5; *ST*, pp. 64–7; *TSA*, Ch 11; of the life, death and resurrection of Jesus of Nazareth in *SCB*, Chs 5, 6; *TSA*, Ch 13; of Christology in *CWS*, Ch 6; *RAS*, pp. 209–14; *SCB*, Ch 7; *ST*, Ch 6; *TSA*, Chs 14, 15; of eschatology in *SCB*, Ch 9.

Books on the topics surveyed in this chapter are legion. It is only possible to give a brief selection of outstanding contemporary texts.

M.J. Borg, *Jesus in Contemporary Scholarship* (Trinity Press International, 1994). On Jesus.

R.E. Brown, *An Introduction to New Testament Christology* (Geoffrey Chapman, 1994). On Christology.

J.G. Dunn, *Christology in the Making* (SCM Press, 1980). On Christology in the New Testament.

W. James, *The Varieties of Religious Experience* (Collins, 1960). The classic text on religious experience in general.

J. Moltmann, *The Theology of Hope* (SCM Press, 1967). On eschatology.

G. O'Collins, *Jesus Risen* (Darton, Longman & Todd, 1987). On the resurrection.

R. Otto, *The Idea of the Holy* (Oxford University Press, 1923). The classic account of the numinous.

W. Pannenberg, *Jesus: God and Man* (SCM Press, 1968). On Christology.

E.P. Sanders, *Jesus and Judaism* (SCM Press, 1985). On Jesus.

A.C. Thiselton, *The Two Horizons* (Eerdmans, 1980). A difficult but important book on hermeneutics.

F.J. Tipler, *The Physics of Immortality* (Macmillan, 1994). On 'physical eschatology'.

N.T. Wright, *Jesus and the Victory of God* (SPCK, 1996). On Jesus.

J.D. Zizioulas, *Being as Communion* (St Vladimir's Seminary Press, 1985). On the Trinity.

7   The World Faiths

Matters relating to the world faith traditions are discussed in *RAS*, pp. 81–92; *SCB*, Ch 10; *ST*, Ch 5; *TSA*, pp. 258–61.

M. Barnes, *Religions in Conversation* (SPCK, 1989). A critique of the exclusivist/pluralist/inclusivist classification.

K. Cragg, *The Christ and the Faiths* (SPCK, 1986). A sympathetic and detailed discussion of world faith traditions, surveyed from a Christian standpoint.

G. D'Costa, *Theology and Religious Pluralism* (Blackwell, 1986). A discussion in terms of the exclusivist/pluralist/inclusivist classification.

H. Küng, *Christianity and the World Religions* (Doubleday, 1986). A sympathetic and detailed discussion of world faith traditions, surveyed from a Christian standpoint.

A. Race, *Christians and Religious Pluralism* (SCM Press, 1983). A discussion in terms of the exclusivist/pluralist/inclusivist classification.

K. Ward, *Images of Eternity* (Darton, Longman & Todd, 1987). Makes a claim to discern some common features present in all the faith traditions.

K. Ward, *Religion and Revelation* (Oxford University Press, 1994). Further discussion of interfaith issues.

K. Ward, *Religion and Creation* (Oxford University Press, 1996). Further discussion of interfaith issues.

8   The Search for Knowledge and Wisdom

Some discussion of ethical issues can be found in *BS*, Ch 9; *CWS*, Ch 7.

I.G. Barbour, *Ethics in an Age of Technology* (SCM Press, 1993). A much more detailed discussion of ethical issues related to science and technology.

Index